Creative Gardens

Creative Gardens

James C. Rose

 REINHOLD PUBLISHING CORPORATION

NEW YORK

CONTENTS

Copyright 1958 · Reinhold Publishing Corporation · Printed in the United States of America · Library of Congress Catalog Card No. 58–7198

Book design by Myron Hall III · Printed by Kingsport Press, Inc. · Bound by Russell-Rutter Co., Inc.

Acknowledgments.

I cannot escape the suspicion that "acknowledgments" are seldom read, and insufficiently noticed — in comparison with the enormous debt they are intended to recognize. I am therefore writing mine by hand in hopes of attracting to them the attention they deserve.

I would like to thank publicly, as I may have neglected to do privately, Mary Davis Gillies of McCall's and Richard Pratt of The Ladies Home Journal for their personal interest in my work; as an expression of that interest, they have made available all the color plates in this book.

My personal debt to the photographers, whose works are identified in a special index, is that I have been permitted to ride along with their very able display of talents. The individual talents are doubly apparent in that I have challenged each of them by a method of design which does not consider the limitations of the camera; their meeting of their challenge can only be described as "noble".

Many projects appearing in these pages were originally shown in the major house and garden periodicals here and abroad, and are also identified in a separate index. I wish to thank each of them for permission to use the photographs here again. I particularly wish to thank House Beautiful for permitting the use of photographs prior to publication in the magazine.

But even more immediately concerned with the book are the publishers who allowed me as nearly complete freedom as it is desirable for an author to have. I cannot conceive of more hearty and intelligent cooperation than I have received from William Wilson Atkin who permitted himself to be used as a sounding board of great sensitivity in all matters of policy and decision.

Myron Hall, in addition to his invaluable assistance with layouts, paid me the unconscious compliment of reading every word in the text — a flattery considered far beyond the call of duty for a layout man, and Professor Charles Rieger, a one time colleague of mine at Columbia, stepped in — with hardly a moment's notice — to produce an outstanding set of sketches which completed the book.

On the mechanical side, but equally important to the presentation, I want to thank David W. De Armond for his good natured patience and meticulous "watchdogging" of all the cuts and engravings, and Mrs. Frances Gildehaus for keeping my spelling and punctuation a secret from the public.

For the faults, of any kind whatever, I beg full credit for myself; after living with them so long, I have come to value imperfections.

PART I

Gardens

In writing a book, as in giving a party, a good host should first enjoy himself; at least one person will then be pleased. I say this not that my own pleasure is so important, but because pleasing is not important at all—especially if it means catering to tastes.

Occasionally, tastes and the creative process fuse into a happy and indistinguishable union. More often, one's personal tastes are a series of likes and dislikes based on experiences already past; the creative is becoming something. Likes and dislikes may tell a great deal about one's preferences in beefsteak, clothes, alcohol, or gardens, but the importance ends right there. These preferences are conditioned by the framework of a society, and private phobias. Like prejudice, they are already with us, preventing something else from happening. The creative is far humbler; it permits nature to perform.

So, while it is not my purpose to offer an unpopular book, and it is even less my purpose to crusade against currently popular taste or the strange rationalizations that underlie it, I think it is important to separate the pursuit of tastes from the realization of the creative process.

This is from one who once believed that some kind of mysterious cure for the ills of the world could be effected if only everyone knew about them. Once, in a student session, I had the effrontery to ask Siegfried Giedeon what he could possibly hope to accomplish with his book, *Space, Time, and Architecture*, when not even one tenth of one percent of the people would ever read it. His simple answer illuminated my thinking irrevocably. He said that he would be quite happy if only one person read and understood his book because every idea started from a nucleus, not the periphery; if it possessed even an element of truth it would prevail whether or not it were popularly accepted. Time, certainly, has proved his thesis. For it would be impossible today to find a magazine article or a major work that did not pay homage, directly or indirectly, to that great book.

I am going to borrow from Giedeon his distinction between transitory and constituent facts. As an historian, he finds that architectural expressions fall into one of these two classes. *Constituent facts* are those tendencies which, when they are suppressed, inevitably reappear producing, in toto, a new tradition. *Transitory facts* are the short-lived novelties—equally the work of forces moving in a period—which lack the stuff of permanence and fail to attach themselves to a new tradition.

This distinction is the essence of understand-

Without Houses

ing our environment and eliminating the confusion of the taste arbiter and the sidewalk critic, who seem to imagine that things are good or bad depending on whether they like or understand them. And I, for one, have always been grateful that this is not true because it would be difficult to conceive of a world in which everything such arbiters or critics did not understand were bad.

Gardens are particularly heir to this kind of whim. They are considered a luxury, like a new hat, that can be worn or not as the occasion demands, but are never truly part of the environmental complex.

Of course, most people would no more admit not liking gardens than they would admit not liking children. For instance, in building a house, it would not occur to anyone to decide whether or not to have a built-in bathroom—although this was a consideration at one time; the question today would simply be how many. But with gardens, there is never quite enough left in the budget; one must give up something to pay for gardens, and it certainly will not be bathrooms—whether we like them or not.

This is particularly strange in the light of older civilizations where it was not unusual to build a garden first, and then find a spot within

it to build a house; but to build a house without a garden at all would be considered a sign of mental illness. And I am not too sure that this is not as good an explanation as any to describe the present scene of development houses—without gardens, without privacy, and without dignity, regardless of the cost range or the number of bathrooms.

I think we can eliminate the cry of poverty or limited budget as an obvious subterfuge—especially when it is accompanied by television, air conditioning, and wall-to-wall carpeting.

The real reason is a complex brewed in a potpourri of commercialism, ad-men, and a sense of urgency about everything else. For a sense of urgency is very necessary to us before we act, and gardens do not seem to have it. I say they do not *seem* to have it because gardens may well be more urgent than we think. But they do not seem to have the kind of urgency in their design, for instance, that is essential to the airplane, which simply will not perform if it violates the laws of flight. Actually, gardens do not perform, either, if they violate the laws of good design, but, unfortunately, this violation is seldom accompanied by a fatal crash. At least, the repercussions take longer to feel. With our gift of unawareness, and docile adaptability to almost any environment, it may be years before we realize that our mechanical ruins were slums all along.

I have just caught myself using that wonderful catch-phrase *good design*, and it seems to pinpoint a flood of schismatic notions about our environment. I think it would be safe to wager that the popular idea of design, good or otherwise, is a container contrived to sell a product —the slick-lined, forward-bent, tail-flying automobile, the stylized house, the flip-top cigarette box. These are obviously transitory expressions of our society, but their chief interest here is that they are completely external—surface attributes that we could not only do without, but might be better off without.

Now, external design, like wallpaper, probably has a place in the scheme of things. There is a whole class of important frivolities, such as Mardi gras, wherein we find great release in making fun of ourselves by separating the outward form of serious endeavor from its inner content, and, with a touch of exaggeration, create a parody. I am all for this kind of stunt— the willful mood, the playful extravagance, even complete nonsense in design, but it must be consciously so. For in awareness is sanity. When we begin to imagine that the manipulation of line and shape, divorced from content, is the same as reality, we are truly lost.

On the other hand, it is not at all remarkable that the laity, continually subjected to this type of design, should conclude that all design is external, an appliqué that, when the going gets rough, can be dispensed with. The theory of separateness is part of the split thinking in a materialistic society. It is extremely convenient, from the split point of view, to remove the creative from its basic role, and relegate it to flip-top boxes; it does not then interfere with building the concrete jungle.

But the creative is made of hardy stuff, although it sometimes has the face of frailty. It is in the hard core of essentials, and has an annoying way of asserting itself, or making its absence felt, in the material world, like the es-

sential negative in an electrical circuit. It is not the materials alone, but their relation to the spaces between that makes a balanced environment. Far from excluding the creative, the material essentials of food, shelter, and clothing are completely bound up with it, for better or worse. It is simply a question of the values with which we want to endow the mundane things of life. But, good or bad, the creative essence is the last to die.

It is only during what is often referred to as "good times" that the hard core of essentials is split into hypothetical necessities and unnecessary luxuries. The great misunderstanding is that the creative is something you contrive to "do" at all; it is really something that you just do not prevent from happening, indeed, the creative is always there—in every thing and every person. It needs only to be revealed. It has nothing to do with luxury or necessity, but it has a lot to do with our readiness to accept it.

In the melee of our civilization, the creative is not an easy thing not to prevent, nor is it easy to exchange for a pot boiler of commercialisms. One must first understand that the hearing ear and the seeing eye are not active organs; they are instead receptacles that simply let the outside world come through. The quality in things is already there in nature and ourselves—confused and hidden, sometimes almost imperceptible, but it is there. The only function of the creative process is to pull back the curtain of obscurity so that everyone ready for it can see.

That is why great and simple art alike has the sense of always having been there. It has. It may just never have reached us before. That is also why it is so hilarious when little "Sam of the art department" tries so desperately to please by manipulating lines and shapes to produce, say, a lipstick case for the commercial Mardi gras. Think of the telephone calls, the tracing paper, the color sketches that go into such a "styling" problem! Think of the bossmen, the ad-men, and the production managers standing there, like Ozymandias, while the lone and level "Sams" stretch far away.

TEA GARDEN

The feeling of a garden capsulated in a space 15- by 20-feet.
This fabric of natural and man-made materials, woven in three dimensions, gives one the sense
of being within something while still out of doors.

Surface: a pattern of brick perforated with grass, pachysandra, day lilies and baby's breath.
Sides: translucent shoji in removable panels, white birch stems, and the common grape vine.
Ceiling: the trellis, overhanging branches, and the sky.

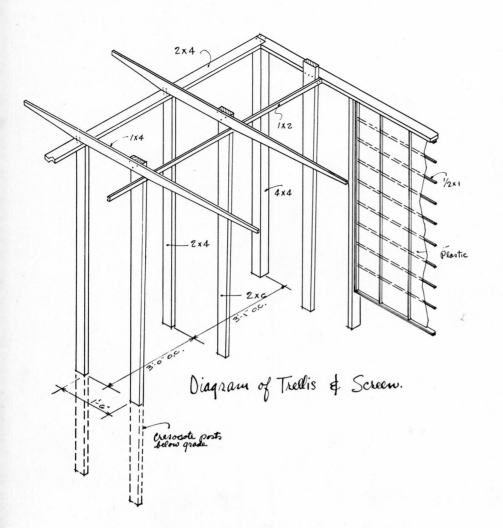

2 x 4

1 x 2

1 x 4

4 x 4

2 x 4

2 x 6

3'-0 oc.

3'-0 oc.

3'-0 oc.

1'-6"

Diagram of Trellis & Screen.

Creosote posts below grade

½ x 1

Plastic

Flexibility is the keynote to this little tea garden. The trellis is a framework for enclosure. It is the structural armature, independent of the screens as it is of planting, but its members are spaced on a three-foot module so that the screens are interchangeable and removable. Any portion of the view can be screened out or let into the garden. The degree of intimacy can be adjusted to the occasion; it can be varied for different times of the day or night, different seasons, the silhouettes caused by sunlight or made by artificial lighting.

Opposite, the screens are removed from one side of the framework to embrace the adjacent lounging area which could be screened off for privacy by replacing shoji panels.

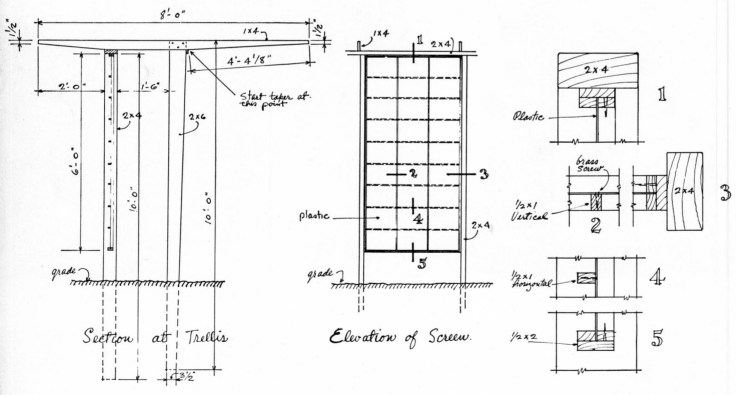

8'-0"

1 x 4

½

½

4'-4 1/8"

Start taper at this point

2'-0"

1'-6"

2 x 4

2 x 6

6'-0"

10'-0"

10'-0"

grade

3½

Section at Trellis

1 x 4

1

2 x 4

2

3

plastic

4

2 x 4

5

grade

Elevation of Screen.

2 x 4

Plastic

1

brass screw

½ x 1 Vertical

2

2 x 4

3

½ x 1 horizontal

4

½ x 2

5

Plastic panels are sandwiched between horizontal and vertical members of the shoji frames for ease of construction, and for the play of light and silhouette. Vertical and horizontal patterns are emphasized differently as the lighting changes.

*Opposite: translucent shojis in place silhouette the unpredictable forms of weeping
mountain ash and obscure the steps to garden entrance shown above. Here, some panels are
removed, so that the interior of the garden is seen as it is approached.*

13

Opposite: view from the entrance with all shojis in place. The distant panel has been removed in picture above showing the view back toward entrance. The surface has a fabric-like quality; grass, pachysandra, and flowers are interwoven with brick.

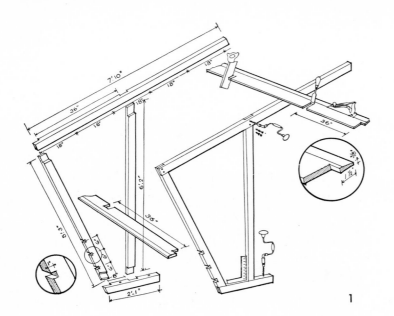

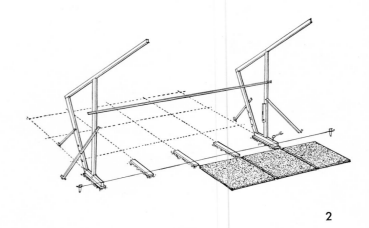

1

2

1 *Construction detail of individual basic unit.* 2 *End units are braced and screwed into sill with lag screws.* 3 *Interior members are placed in position and adjusted to exact three-foot spacing on center.* 4 *Top and side louvers are placed in position and held by finishing nails. Trellis arch is screwed to sill.*

A

B

C

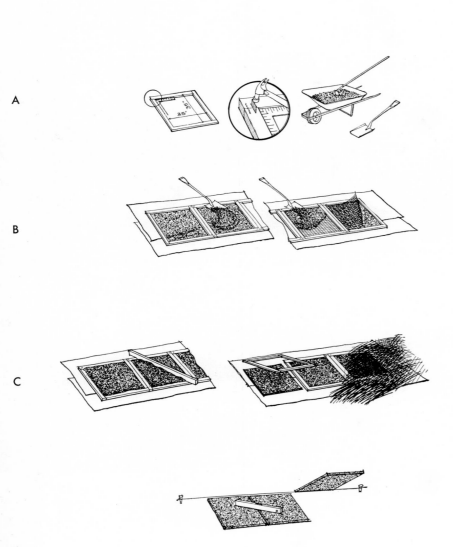

D

E

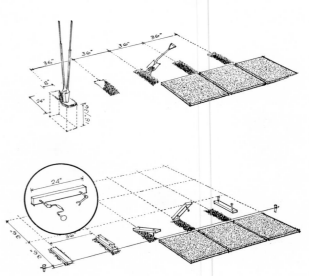

A   *Frames are 35 × 35″ inside dimension (to allow for paving joints), and a depth of one inch.*

B   *Bottom of form is sprinkled with colored pebbles for texture, and frames half filled with concrete mix.*
Turkey wire is then inserted, snugly fitting the corners, and the frames filled completely.

C   *The concrete is leveled and allowed to cure under straw. The frames are then removed.*

D   *This one-inch thin wafer of concrete is then set in its garden position on four inches of leveled sand—textured side up. Footings are dug, filled with concrete to below frost line.*

E   *Two-by-four sills are lag-screwed into concrete while it is still green. The sills are then worked into the concrete until they are level with each other, and three feet from center to center.*

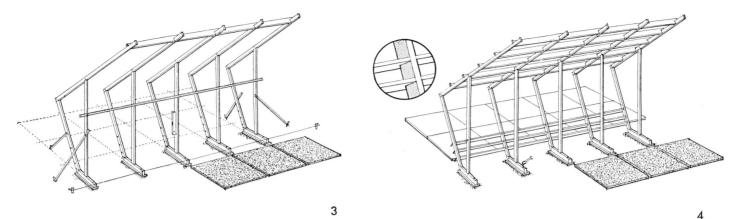

Modular Gardens

In 1946, the Ladies Home Journal commissioned a series of small gardens, including the one just described. The sole interest of the magazine was in sensationally "dreamy" photographs for publication; if the pictures could be procured without the gardens, so much the better. It was even seriously suggested that the gardens might be painted on a large canvas in the background, and photographed, Hollywood fashion, with a realistically constructed foreground to carry a sense of verisimilitude. The theory was that things appear more glamorous if they are unattainable, and if you are unable to tell how they are accomplished.

This had a certain merit from the point of view of the magazine, but I could not bring myself to subscribe to the cloudland school of accomplishing the unusual, because simply to be sensible about gardens is so unusual that it almost amounts to sensationalism.

I proposed a modular system of standardized garden units including trellis members, walls and space dividers, paving, pools, and plant forms. Whatever this proposal may have lacked in "glamour," it made up for in clarity and economy; for once such a system had been worked out, the parts could be reassembled and reused in an almost infinite variety of space patterns. In the long run it would be as cheap or cheaper than painting scenes on canvas, considering that time, labor, and photography would be spent on either. It also gave an opportunity to study the problems of the small garden at full scale and in many variations under controlled conditions. The idea had within it the possibility of mass reproduction, which

meant that it could be economically applied to the most common landscape problem—the average home grounds. But more important, it established a discipline. It is sometimes difficult to accept self-imposed disciplines; they are too often regarded as needless shackles to liberty rather than a bridge to freedom, but it is literally impossible, in dealing with the amorphous and elusive stuff of gardens, to create an effective landscape without them. Here is a set of modular parts worked out for this prosaic, but essential purpose.

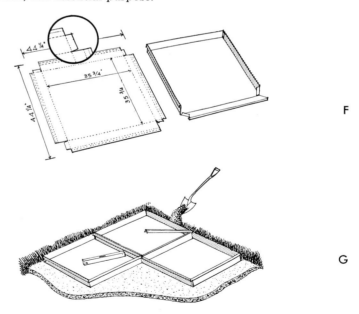

F

G

F   *Pool pans, made in the same module, are interchangeable with the paving blocks. To avoid costly plumbing, the units are filled with a hose and emptied by hand, although drains and circulating water are possible.*
G   *The pans are painted and set on a four-inch bed of sand—which must be absolutely level.*

Detail of wood scaffolding with annual vine.

Garden space created by adaptation of modular parts and planting. Fish net, woven with varicolored ribbon strips in camouflage pattern, is used as a draw curtain. Modular trellis, same as color detail shown opposite, and wood scaffolding form the armature of the space—reemphasized by a systematic planting of plant forms in planes of different heights above and below the eye level. Surface of modular paving, pool pans, and open spaces complete the scheme.

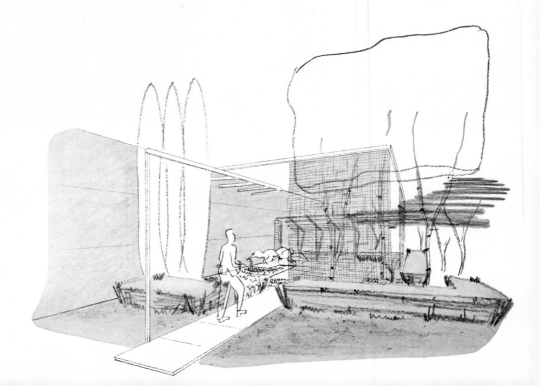

Trial assembly of modular parts: constructed trellis, precast concrete squares, and prefabricated pool pans. Perforations are left in the pattern for modular planting and sand pit.

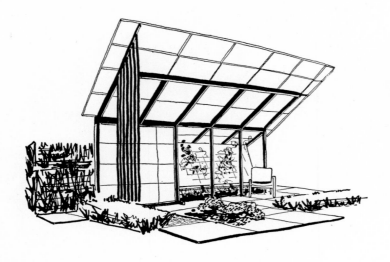

When I was a student in the School of Design at Harvard, the split between architecture and landscape architecture was clearly defined. The landscape architects were on the ground floor, although I draw no inference from this, and the architects were on the second floor—of the same building, however.

One of the irritations of student life was that the architects developed the habit of rushing downstairs, drawings in hand, a few minutes before their problems were due, demanding that the landscapers draw in some shrubbery, or "a little garden" to make their buildings seem less formidable. I put up with this nonsense for nearly a full semester, and then designed a little garden unencumbered by any buildings. At the strategic moment, when the architects were thoroughly engrossed in their own parabolas, I dashed upstairs and asked them to design a building for my garden.

The reaction was not at all what I had expected; the architects were insulted, but I think they missed the point because they are still, at the eleventh hour, looking for a landscape to suit their buildings.

Paradoxically, the first commission I received after World War II was to design a series of little gardens without houses. I was delighted because in a period of diffusion, when paintings are done mainly for museum exhibition, and sculpture must have a setting built for it instead of being designed for the location, and houses are so often designed as a neat little package without regard to site, landscape, or gardens, it does not seem unreasonable to isolate the garden itself for experiment. It might even be healthy to come back to the house from that point of view.

In the beginning, I had the fond hope of developing a *system* for building small gardens rather than just producing a series of individual projects. The key to this seemed to be that each of the parts would have a common denominator, so that they could be used interchangeably and reassembled in a variety of ways, like an Erector set. It would remain only to find the proper combination to suit a specific condition. The materials were to be of common stuff, universally available, and the parts easily fabricated at the local shop by local mechanics.

At first glance, the system seemed like a perfect one to eliminate at least part of a landscape architect's service, I was quite happy for this because a service that owes its existence to the pat "professional secret" is no service at all once the secret is discovered, and any real professional would rather go on to new problems. It also seemed to be a legitimate answer to the how-to-do-it school since it embraced the whole problem, instead of specifics, and reduced it to an intelligent assembly of parts. In my mind, it represented a discipline which might help the amateur to proceed from a solid basis of structure instead of being tempted by amorphous whisps of remembered "effects."

The tendency in the homemade landscape is

to be too specific and direct—on the practical side, to plant a tree where shade is needed, to mark off an area and fill it with concrete and flagstone for a terrace, to build a fence where it screens out the neighbor or keeps the dog in; on the aesthetic side, to plant a willow by the pool, or, perhaps, white birches to reflect in it. This all seems like virtuous procedure and good business sense. It is. But it seldom produces gardens—not creative gardens—for the result is only the sum total of the individual "effects." It is similar to what occurs in photographs. However beautiful or factual they may be, you get just one point of view under one set of conditions. And this is not the purpose or the promise of creative gardens.

More is gained by indirection than at first meets the eye or is easy to admit. I always find it a minor miracle the way a chance remark or a quick, sidelong glance can reveal a whole new world of experience. Such a miracle happened to me one day when an old professor of mine made what may have been a well calculated remark but which seemed very casual. Placing first one index finger in the air and then the other he said, "One and one are two—that's business." Then he drew his two fingers together leaving a space exactly the width of each. "One and one are three," he continued, "that's art." I was quite impressed, but it was a time before I realized the full impact of this remark. I began, finally, to discover that one and one could add up to more than three—to

anything you wanted them to—even to infinity.

In applying this principle to gardens, it is impossible to begin with the specific—the mud that is being tracked into the living room, the ugly foundation that "cries out" to be covered. These are symptoms. The effort spent on treating them specifically is patchwork, and as patchwork, it usually succeeds only in attracting more attention to the original problem.

Particularly in the instance of the ugly foundation, the direct approach has been tried for generations to no avail. Statistics will bear me out that millions are spent each year in attempts to cover this specific mistake with foliage of all kinds, yet with the house looming out of the ground, it looks like parsley at the base of a turkey. Except that the ugly foundation is an inexcusable fault in building construction, once you have it the problem is similar to that of having a large nose: you either live with it, resort to reconstruction in the form of surgery, or do something to attract attention to other parts. You do not hang a bell on it to cover it up.

I do not mean to over emphasize the ugly foundation for it is only one problem, and not necessarily the worst. I am more concerned here with a method for handling the immovable condition whatever it may be; and directing attention to other parts more attractive, or at least less unattractive, is the clue. It can be done with unbelievable ease if one can resist making the direct attack. This was the purpose in developing a *system* of modular gardens. By such a system, one could avoid the offending right eye, so to speak, if he were unwilling to pluck it out. The reason is that by creating new space the offending part is absorbed in it, and its special importance is thereby diminished.

The annoying thing about problems of this kind is that they are created by some one else, and inherited by the landscape architect. Their solution is a cross between camouflage and cosmetology which have little to do with land planning, space, or gardens. They simply represent another series of obstacles in the way of the final objective.

Annoying as it may be, when one realizes how easily man-made obstacles could have been avoided, it is understandable that they were not. It is understandable because, I have discovered, most people do not have the faintest notion of what the final objective is. They do not know what a landscape is. They do not know what a garden is.

A garden is an experience. It is not flowers, or plants of any kind. It is not flagstone, brick, grass, or pebbles. It is not a barbeque, or a Fiberglas screen. It is an experience. If it were possible to distill the essence of a garden, I think it would be the sense of being within something while still out of doors. That is the substance of it; for until you have that, you do not have a garden at all.

The difficulty with most so-called gardens is that they are flat. They never get over the hurdle of the ground plane. They are patterns to be observed, instead of space to be experienced. This seems to me to result entirely from a habit of thinking. It is like the old fashioned conundrum: how can you make four equilateral triangles out of six matches of the same length? The earthbound will struggle eternally on a flat plane without getting the answer because the answer lies in thinking in volume.

Obviously, as many sins can be committed in volume as in pattern—in fact, more, because volume includes pattern. What makes it good? I believe it is the relationship between what I like to call the positive and the negative elements—the solid and the void, materials and space. These are arranged, like the professor's fingers, so that they not only create an integral void or space, but together, they fuse to become something new. This could become nothing more than an academic exercise if it were done without further purpose. But there is a further purpose and that is to create a frame of reference which will make our perception of nature more acute. The whole purpose is nothing more than this; and this is an infinity.

The question of how much space you need to capture infinity falls into that large category of hysterical questions: how long should a man's legs be, how deep is a well, how wide is a door? As G. K. Chesterton once pointed out in referring to the enormous rock portraits of our presidents in the desert, things can be too large as well as too small for human perception, and, he warned, if we did not curb our enthusiasm for largeness we would find whole villages growing up on the eyebrow of Abraham Lincoln.

Obviously, there is an irreducible minimum in which infinity can be captured in a garden. There must be enough space for the experience to happen to a person or group, and enough space for the elements that compose it. But, like the little girl who observed that it is easier to pronounce large words than small ones, there are a great many truths that seem absurd on the face of them, and the difficulty of attracting infinity in a tiny garden space is one of these truths. The amateur and the student should always begin with a large canvas and a complex of elements until he learns what the essence is. I have found it helpful to think of a garden as sculpture. Not sculpture in the ordinary sense of an object to be viewed. But sculpture that is large enough and perforated enough to walk through. And open enough to present no barrier to movement, and broken enough to guide the experience which is essentially a communion with the sky.

This is a garden.

Metamorphosis: the following pages demonstrate the range and flexibility of a modular system in developing an idea from its inception to final form and subsequent reinterpretation. Each of these garden "incidents" is composed of precisely the same parts in varying arrangements. Basic to each is the angular trellis, 3-foot square paving blocks of precast and colored concrete, and standard reflecting pool 3- by 3-feet. The planting beds can be varied for seasonal effect by lifting the paving sections and setting flowers in their place. When the effect is past, the flowers can be removed and the paving restored. One might use perennials or ground cover in permanent beds and annuals in the seasonal beds, but since the limits are well defined by paving, the appearence is always well kept.

Original sketches showing two views of a pool garden based on a 3-foot module. All elements, including type and placement of furniture, are shown in detail and exact size to scale.

Sketches were developed from scale models and plans, showing the space relationships between plant forms, trellis, fence, and ground surface treatment. The modular parts, as organized separately, are shown opposite to demonstrate their interlocking relation. The parts are fitted together with each part and open space indispensable to the other.

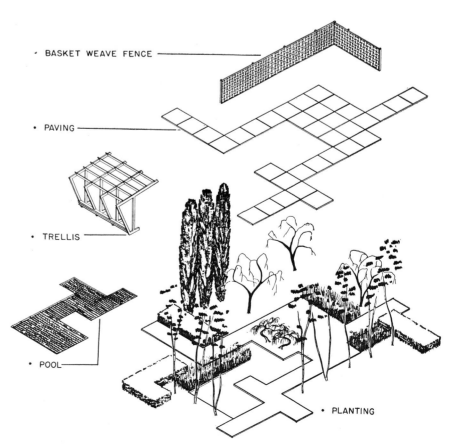

· BASKET WEAVE FENCE

· PAVING

· TRELLIS

· POOL

· PLANTING

Semi-finals: with pool pans and paving squares in place, the spring planting scheme is tested in color and time of bloom. Garden furniture, later arranged as shown in original sketches, is used here to study scale.

A mock-up of actual garden shown opposite. 3- by 3-foot squares of cardboard are used instead of concrete for ease in handling—fence and small planting in tentative positions to study relationships and camera angles. The final placement of all elements turned out to be best as originally suggested in sketches.

Reinterpretation: the identical space scheme, or armature, as shown on preceding pages.
The same basic sense of volume and succession of planes in both planting and
structure are retained, but new surface patterns, furniture, and flowers give a
different feeling within the same space.

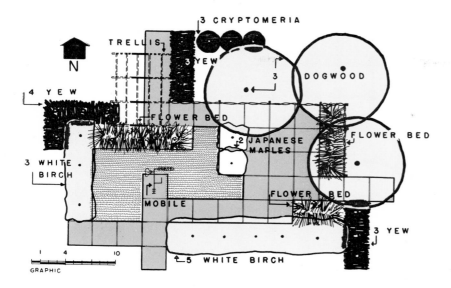

Basic modular scheme with geometric pattern.

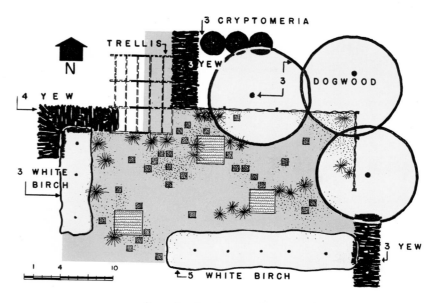

Same basic scheme reinterpreted.

In the reinterpretation of the basic space scheme, pulverized brick and railroad tie cross sections in a casual pattern replace the 3- by 3-feet concrete square paving. The pool pans are raised and dispersed in pattern. The flower scheme, essentially iris, is brought out of individual beds and diffused. Furniture is more sophisticated in style and arrangement.

An enormous sense of space is created in an area measuring 20′ × 30′.

Morning Glory Shelter

Morning glories have a habit of opening with the earliest sun, and closing an hour later if still exposed. On gloomy days, or if brought indoors, the blooms will last all day. This shelter is designed to trick them into remaining open. It faces just north of east, with a wide projecting roof sloping upward to the morning sun. The early light penetrates, opening the flowers, and then, as the sun moves to the west and south, the flowers are protected from its rays by the translucent roof and shojis. During the day, the roof and shojis glow with an iridescent light that is broken by the sun casting an exotic, ever-changing pattern of silhouetted plant forms. Within the shelter, the atmosphere is cool during the day, as in the shade of a tree. The late afternoon sun sparkles on the pool surface, and the morning glories are still in bloom.

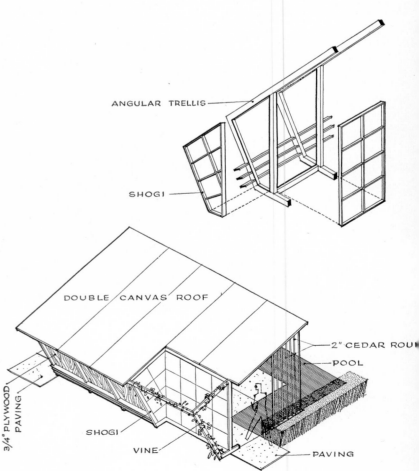

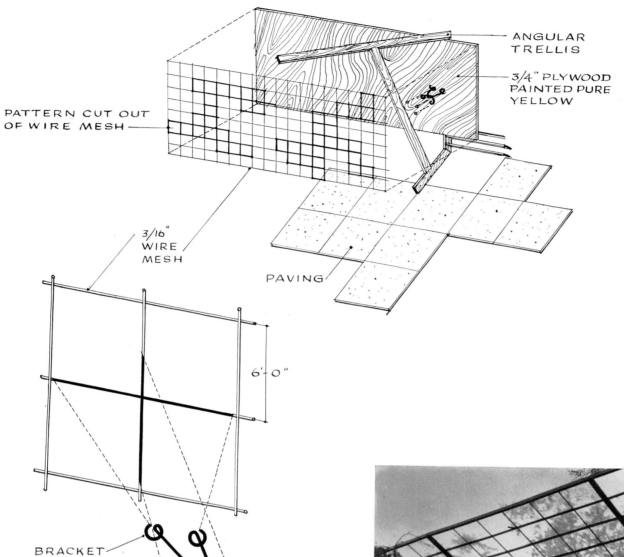

ANGULAR
TRELLIS

3/4" PLYWOOD
PAINTED PURE
YELLOW

PATTERN CUT OUT
OF WIRE MESH

3/16"
WIRE
MESH

PAVING

6'-0"

BRACKET

A variation of the modular garden takes the form of a garden shelter. Based on the angular trellis, it is composed of common materials—painted plywood and concrete reinforcing wire mesh, translucent plastic, canvas, paving squares, sheet metal water pans, and modular planting. Flowers are petunias and morning glories.

Boudoir garden off bath and dressing rooms—a nicety that is rare in the modern scheme, but an integral part of ancient oriental living. Here the precast concrete squares are interrupted by pool pans in a modular arrangement. One paving square is raised to serve as a table top. A translucent wall shields this garden from the rest of the landscape, and a curtain drawn across the dressing room and bath give complete privacy while the trellis and weeping Mountain Ash tree contribute to the feeling of enclosure. The boudoir table, with mirror, at left, and crocheted hammock at right suggest relaxed and comfortable living.

BOUDOIR GARDEN

This "garden without a house" was built to be photographed, and then torn down. It served admirably the purpose of the *Ladies Home Journal* to demonstrate the idea of garden glamour in narcissistic terms of a boudoir. The dream quality hoped for by the magazine is accomplished in reality without resorting to theatrical illusion either in construction or photography. The mockup describes and suggests, in a practical vocabulary, the flexibility of modular system which, far from a handicap to glamour, became a productive discipline to that end. For true glamour is in the economy of effort to effect—not in shadowy illusion.

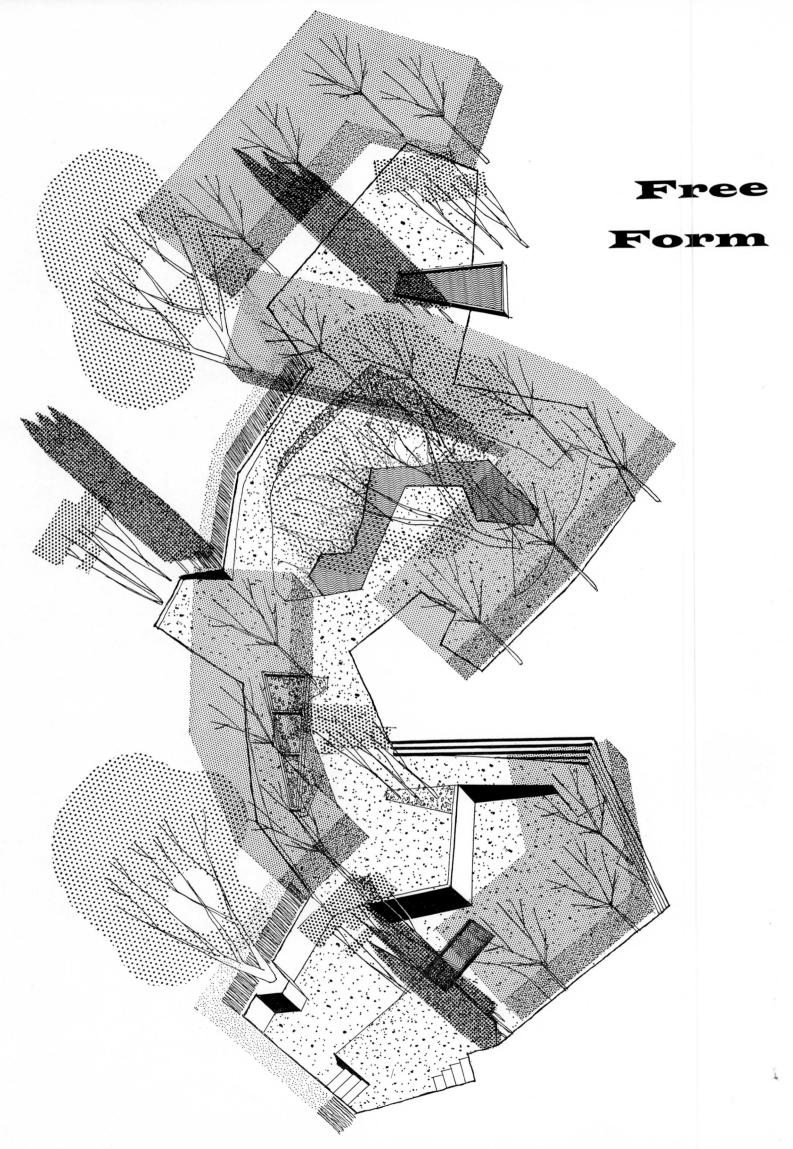

Free Form

The painfully corseted lady who put a kimono over her corset to "loosen things up a bit" is similar to what passes for free form today. It is completely free in that its form has nothing to do with what is inside. The curvilinear outline of a terrace, the path that snakes its way through the grass, the inevitable kidney shaped pool rival only the whitewashed stones along the driveway, the wagon wheel, and the rubber tire filled with petunias in their naïve attempts to get an "effect." These efforts have one thing in common—they start with a stillborn notion of form instead of allowing it to evolve.

Originally, free form, as opposed to geometric form, was an attempt to replace the arbitrary line and the rectilinear shape with a less mechanical concept that would reveal more the quality and kind of form that evolves in nature. If this is so, one can do no better than to learn from nature what the form is and how it came about.

Probably one of the best examples of land formation in nature is made by the meandering stream that cuts its way through an almost level field. The line is serpentine because of the flatness of the land. It is finding its way with a powerful suggestion of movement, but it is not a lone or isolated line independent of its surroundings. The stream is carving the land, cutting peninsulas of projecting and receding shapes. The stream itself is widening and narrowing, depending on the hardness of the adjacent ground and the force of the water. If the field flattens, the water body widens, and little islands or drifts of land appear in a field of water completing the cycle of reversal—positive to negative, land to water. Each, the land and the water, maintains its own integrity while acting on and modifying the other until a new thing appears which is not either or even both of the others.

This oneness evolving from the fusion and interplay of materials is characteristic of good form anywhere. It makes little difference whether the materials are hard and square cut, or fluid and amorphous in shape—the principle will be the same.

Take any level piece of ground. Bring a man on to it, and its pattern is immediately modified; it becomes partly a man-pattern reflecting his movements and activity. Let us say you decide to anticipate his movements. You can plot paths. If you think of paths only, the land will be divided into a kind of patchwork because every line will automatically leave segments of one shape or another. Usually neglected, these segments are the negative elements; the path itself, the positive. Each is equally important to fusion. You design the negative while introducing the positive. The tendency is to settle for a mechanically arrived at positive line which answers only the "path" problem, and ignores total fusion.

This simple principle, projected into community planning, accounts for our tendency to design slums with such immediate facility. We see only the positive, and ignore the spaces in between. It is a tendency which we must unlearn before good planning is possible.

When a third dimension is introduced, we are dealing with height and contour, as in a sphere, as well as pattern. We are dealing with the elements of enclosure—the sense of being within something.

I would choose the sand or gravel pit as an illustration because these are natural forms crudely modified by man: the excavated hills form a crescent shape which has some of the characteristics of sculpture. The crescent line is, again, caused indirectly by the cut made in the earth, and a shadow is cast by the sun over its concave slope making a continually moving line. Thus, we have an extension of pattern into volume with a by-product of both a stabile and a mobile line. The forms are integral with their substance, and line follows form.

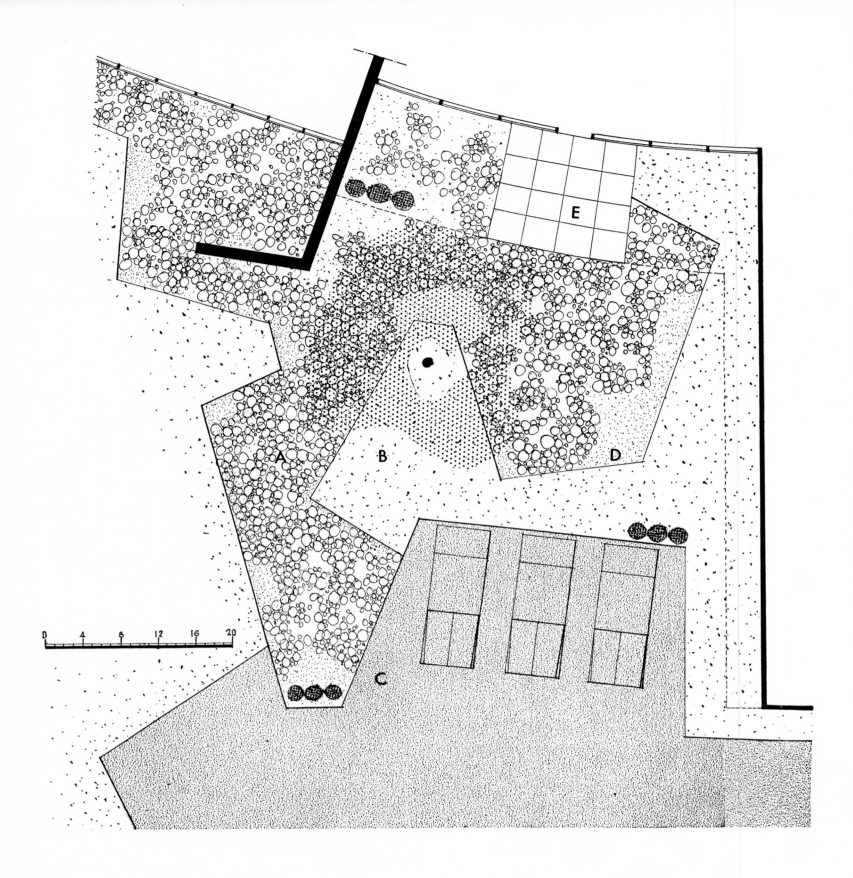

Pattern in Free Form

Free form pattern as applied to the entrance court of a large house. The ground cover area (B) separates the blacktop parking area (C) from the more gardenesque treatment close to house. Guests enter over wood disk area (A) around and under spreading tree planted in B to paved apron (E) under canopy at entrance door.

The wood disks range in size from six to thirty inches and are generalized, rather than path-like, in a field of ochre pebbles. Each form interlocks with every other to create a unity of positive and negative elements. The space objectives— separation and integration in terms of the special problem—seem to happen naturally. 1957

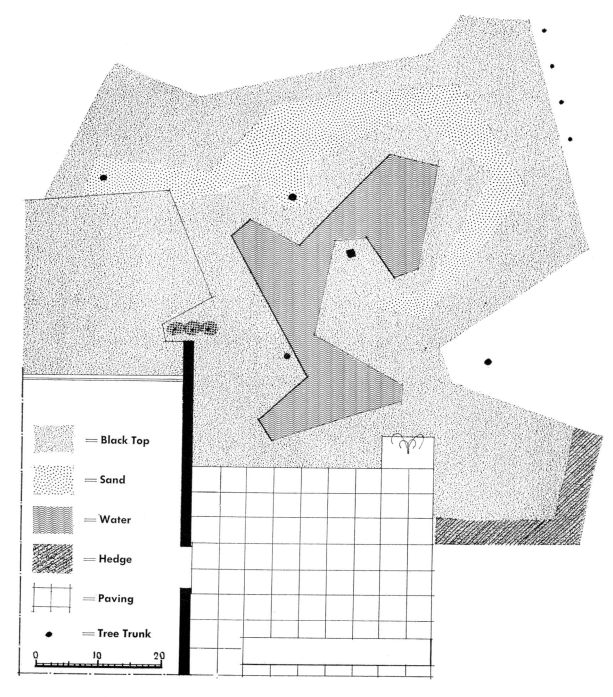

	= Black Top
	= Sand
	= Water
	= Hedge
	= Paving
●	= Tree Trunk

0   10   20

Interlocking forms, in pattern of children's play space, off small paved terrace

A combination of rigid and free forms in the pattern of the children's maze, which is projected into the third dimension on next page.

CHILDREN'S MAZE, a fantasy

Originally conceived as a protest against statues in the park, the intention here was to develop a park-scale civic monument which, instead of providing for memorial statues, would have the quality of sculpture within it-itself, and would be an animated expression, in landscape forms, of the activity it housed.

The maze, an ancient and honorable landscape form, has found its expression in most periods of history, but seldom, if ever, has it been interpreted in the contemporary idiom.

This particular maze is a study of free and geometric forms, in counterpoint patterns—portions of which are projected into the third dimension to create a plastic system of baffles. The literary connotation is an Oz-like land of amazement for children. Inpenetrable arrangements of plantings and water, flower beds, walls, and fences interrupt their progress toward the Wizzard. They encounter new and pleasant spaces while the Wizzard, waiting at their objective, confuses and misdirects their journey, but it is necessary to make a complete circuit of the area to arrive at the shelter top where the total pattern can be seen. 1939

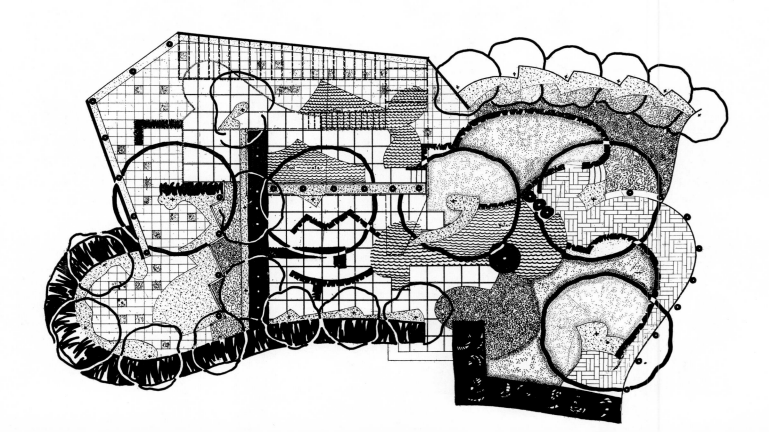

The plan of a maze in the gardens of Versailles (right) invites comparison with plan of children's maze (opposite, lower left). Early Roman and Elizabethan English mazes were extremely symmetrical garden labyrinths following a set pattern as rigid as that of a sonnet. The Versailles maze shown here breaks considerably with traditional form, while retaining some rigidity. The American Indian corn mazes and the Zulu labyrinths were considerably freer in pattern.

The perspective views of children's maze (below and opposite) demonstrate the reorientation of forms to express the maze in a contemporary space idiom.

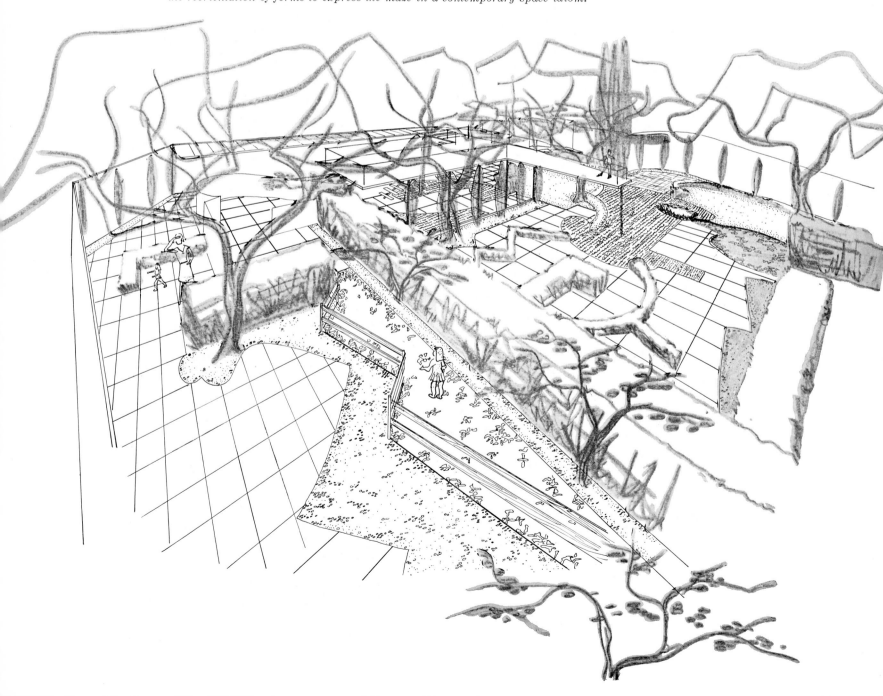

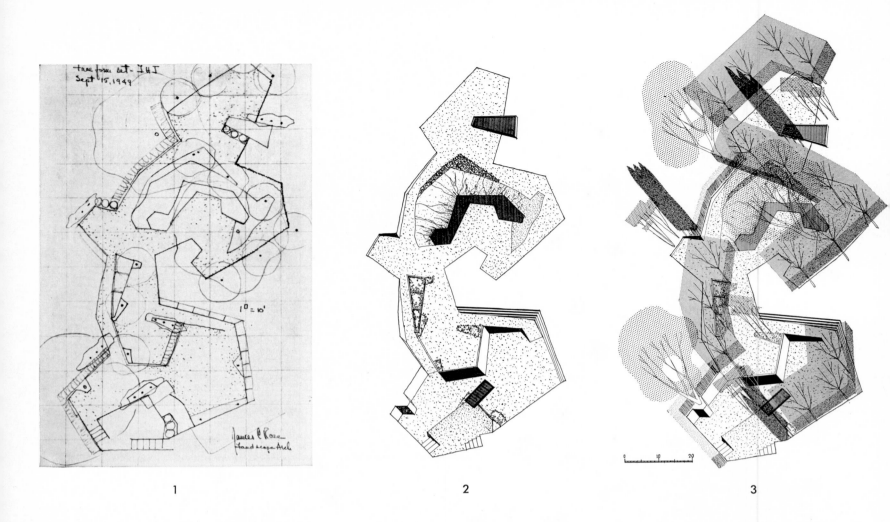

1

2

3

This project was drawn first with a bulldozer on the ground before any drawings were made on paper. The forms were then plotted to scale on paper and shaped as shown in sketch #1. The modifications were then made on the ground. Sketch #2 is a presentation drawing to show ground forms, levels, and surfaces. Sketch #3 describes the planting in relation to ground forms, and illustrates an interspatial rhythm in planting consistent with, and emphasizing, the ground modeling.

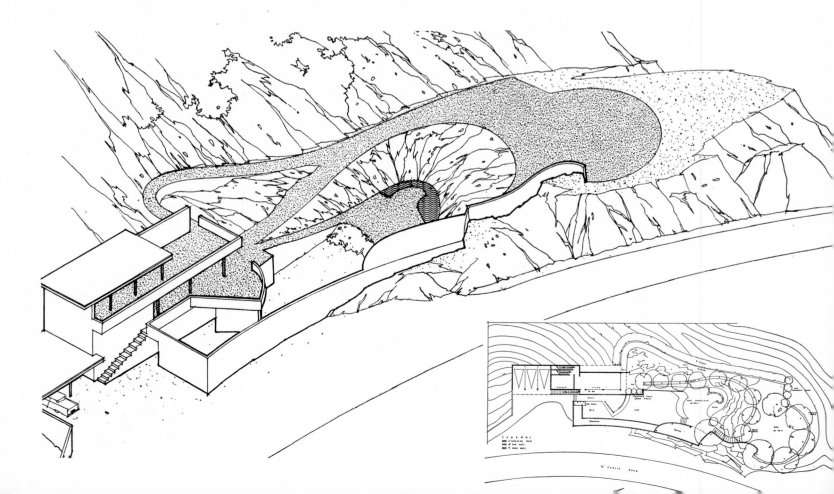

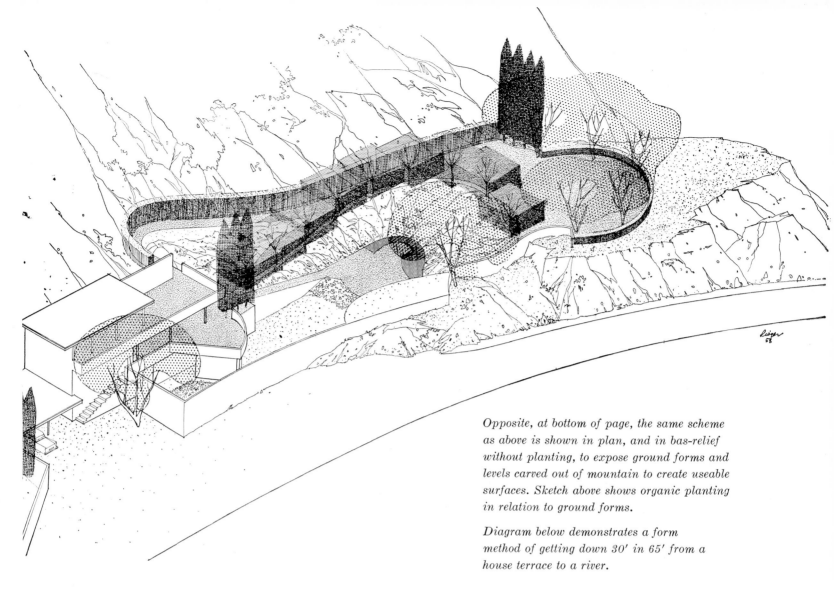

Opposite, at bottom of page, the same scheme as above is shown in plan, and in bas-relief without planting, to expose ground forms and levels carved out of mountain to create useable surfaces. Sketch above shows organic planting in relation to ground forms.

Diagram below demonstrates a form method of getting down 30' in 65' from a house terrace to a river.

FREE FORM
IN THREE DIMENSIONS

In the past few decades a great deal of false security has been built up in the public mind about the value of having a plan "on paper." But in a three dimensional garden, a "plan" has the same limitations that it would have for sculpture. The "plan" gives only a two dimensional picture which requires skillful interpretation—especially in planting where the elements are growing, and the same plant, by name, may be found in many different forms and sizes. Workmen and clients alike are frequently amazed by the apparent discrepancy between the flat plan and its ultimate interpretation in volume.

0   5   10

Food is prepared and cooked on the opposite side of the wing ready to serve at the swivel table.

Occasionally, a house is designed so obliviously that it is impossible to tie the landscape to it at any point, and a gimmick is necessary to provide landscape interest. It is usually better if such a gimmick is structurally separate from the house to avoid a strained connection. Here is a three-way space divider designed as a tripod that can be set on any level ground. Its function is to provide for the specific activities of herb and vegetable gardening, food preparation, and relaxation in the cultivated landscape.

The Garden Maker

The tripod "gimmick" is set down in an orchard paved with modular concrete squares. This is the growing area for vegetables, fruit, and herbs—visible, but separated from the rest by the flying wing and pool pans set in the paving.

After the meal, relax
in the flower garden.

Houses Plus

The Planned

We hear a great deal of high-sounding talk these days in the house and garden magazines about "expressing your individuality," "togetherness," and "perfect privacy" in your own back yard. No one ever mentions—least of all the magazines—the very real and highly fortified obstacles to any semblance of individuality, integration, or privacy in the average community. These obstacles are of a very curious type because each one is thoroughly planned, or at least sanctioned, in the most orderly and democratic way. Each has its own high-sounding motive, and is backed either by custom or law just as if the ends were desirable.

Each of the problems is separately considered from widely different points of view, and, when they are brought together, they represent a series of conflicts and contradictions thrown directly in the lap of the homeowner who is still aglow from the color pages of the magazine.

The House and Its Economies

The house itself has come in to a great deal of publicity in recent years. In a sense, it has taken the center of the stage, and that was quite a necessary step in the process of development. But, by and large, it also has been studied in an isolated way, not so much in a test tube, so to speak, as under a bell jar.

It has been presented as a show piece, under glass, first by the great innovating architects at the turn of the century as an integrated thing in itself. Later, by the second and third generations of architects with less vision and talent, but an enormous facility at stringing together the clichés in a convincing manner. And finally by the builder who made his own nauseating interpretation, based on sales gimmicks, which resulted in the picture window, the ranch house, the split level, and lately, something known as the cathedral living room.

Regardless of quality or motive, these efforts have one thing in common—they are complete entities in themselves. They lack the broad principle, immediate flexibility, and intelligent standardization that would permit them to adapt comfortably to the special conditions of the site.

Far too much has been made of virtuosity in domestic architecture, and we have lost sight of the fact that it is essentially a utility core with a protective shell. The rest is the site and the guided performance of nature.

When this package or entity is brought down to the point of view of the owner, some very

Gardens
Schizophrenia

curious things happen. He is not prepared to think of his house as an incident in the landscape, or an incident in anything else, for that matter. It is a costly and heroic attempt to gain shelter in the face of gargantuan conflicts: the developer, the builder, the architect, the adman, the decorator, and his own inadequacies. He is far more likely to take refuge in the comforting notion that this *is* an entity, and therefore can end somewhere, than he is likely to become expansive, at a time like this, and experiment with his relation to nature.

The Average Lot and Its Restrictions

If you told the average owner that he could not build a wall, a fence, or a trellis wherever he wanted to on his own property, you would have to be prepared for a mild explosion. Upon investigation, he would find that in practically all communities it is forbidden to build any structure including walls, fences, or trellises, over four feet in height, outside the so-called setback lines. Now, the set-back lines will vary somewhat in each community and with each piece of property, depending on its size, whether it is a corner or interior lot, and other special

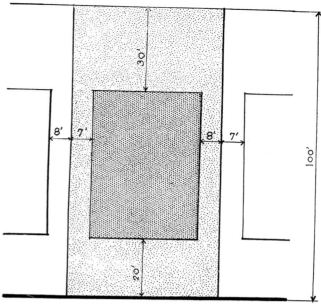

Total Lot Area (Light grey): 5,000 sq ft
Building Area (Dark grey): 1,750 sq ft or 35% of the lot

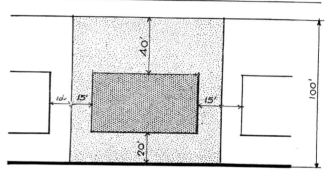

Total Lot Area (Light grey): 10,000 sq ft or approx. ¼ acre
Building Area (Dark grey): 2,800 sq ft or 28% of the lot

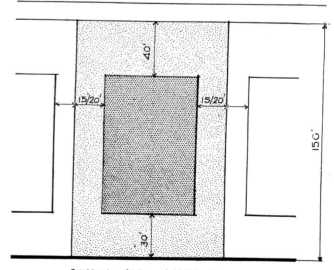

Total Lot Area (Light grey): 15,000 sq ft
Building Area (Dark grey): 4,800 sq ft or 32% of the lot

Archaic setback laws in the United States, while mechanically preserving open area, defeat the integration of interior and exterior space. "House" location on the lot is arbitrarily dictated without regard to view, exposure, or orientation. The "landscape" is what is left over—usually narrow strips between house and property line; unuseable, but must be maintained by the owner. Of the average suburban lot, 70% becomes, in effect, community space for lack of integrated privacy, although privately owned and highly taxed.

conditions. But, in general, the total effect is that only thirty to forty-five percent of any lot can be used for building of any kind.

The purpose is to preserve open space in the community. This sounds like an admirable objective, and it is. The difficulty is that it places all the responsibility for, and the maintenance of, these open spaces on the individual land owner while, in effect, it is a community benefit. It is a method of substituting private restrictions for community planning. And its influence on the living quality, privacy, and useableness of the average house and lot is probably greater than the influence of the past five generations of architects and landscape architects combined.

1 It dictates the location of a house on the small lot regardless of the terrain, view, orientation, or individual preference.

2 It precludes the possibility of any real privacy, in the sense of a dwelling, beyond the set-back line.

3 A great portion of the fifty-five to seventy percent of the property beyond the set-back lines is essentially public domain, unless extensive landscaping is undertaken, although the private owner is required to maintain and pay taxes on this property.

4 The vistas of domestic architecture and landscape architecture, to say nothing of community planning, are retarded essentially to the colonial concept of house plus yard.

Dollar Planning of the Land

Recently, I had an urgent call from a developer. He needed the services of a landscape architect immediately because he was planning to show his houses to the public in two weeks.

When I arrived on the site, I was quite amazed. It was not the flat little entanglement of streets, telephone poles, and buildings I had expected. It was a hillside with a magnificent view of the valley such as one has become accustomed to expect only on a far Pacific island.

I was momentarily impressed—until we began the tour. Then I discovered that this whole beautiful piece of property—the flats and slopes alike had been cut up, like a melon, the only guide being to get as many pieces out of it as the law would allow. Thus, while it was not exactly a gridiron layout, the only criteria had been that a "lot" was made up of a pre-determined number of square feet.

However, the developer was not unaware of the sales potential of a beautiful site. He had built only three houses in scattered locations so that the prospective buyer would still sense the beauty of the original tract, without realizing what would happen to it when the property was finally fitted to a stock model house every hundred feet. In fact, the buyer's unawareness was the developer's frankly admitted capital gain.

The three "model" houses already built must have been drawn from a lottery for, with all their manic-depressive splits in level, they bore not the slightest relation to the ups and downs of the land. Furthermore, to get enough level land to build such a house on such a lot, the developer found it necessary to blast and bulldoze every square inch until what had been woodland was now a barren declivity of shale coming into a level area just large enough for the house, and then another declivity into the next lot. After all this effort, when you finally got into the house, you might just as well have been in Flatbush. The only spot where you could sense the drama in the site, was from the narrow ledge at the front door. Once inside the house, you might peep at the view from behind decorator's curtains, but you could approach it only through an obstacle course of interior levels back to the narrow ledge at the front door.

My job was to "landscape" it. The developer said he felt he needed a real expert, and I quite agreed with this, but since I was being paid for consultation, I pointed out that the real landscaping had already been "done." And what had not been "done" by the landscaping, had been "done" by the house.

He took this rather good naturedly, I

thought, like a parent amused by the antics of his spoiled child, but I soon found out that what he really wanted from me was to dress it up in some sort of planting that would make it more saleable. He was prepared to spend an unreasonable sum, and I had to agree that it could be made to look very pretty, but unuseable still, because every avenue of communication between the site, the landscaping, the house, and the occupant had been blocked in irrevocable terms. This was of no importance. "They won't realize that until they've lived there a year," he said.

I came away with several impressions. First of all, this was not an evil man. He was acting in a thoroughly acceptable way, according to his standards, with even a little of the pioneer spirit, and pride in being a builder. The buyer

was fair game in his code, and he knew the buyer well enough to realize that if he did not win him with chicanery, his competitor would. At least, he was not a hypocrite.

What I resented most was that here I could see the new beginning of an old familiar pattern—not an isolated instance—but an accepted method of developing the land. Aside from the fact that it has happened and is happening in every hamlet throughout the country, the terrifying part of it is that the method is a dead end—an ingrowing kind of disease, and like a disease, it can only proceed in the direction of spoil. The recipe is simple: first, spoil the land by slicing it in particles that will bring the most dollars, add any house that has sufficient selling gimmicks to each slice, and garnish with "landscaping."

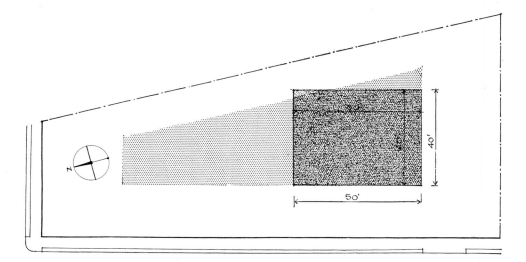

Due to set back restrictions, less than 35% of this lot could be built on (area shown in light grey). A conventional house of 2000 square feet could fit only in the position shown in dark grey at right. The dull island of "house" in a sea of public domain is characteristic of the American suburb.

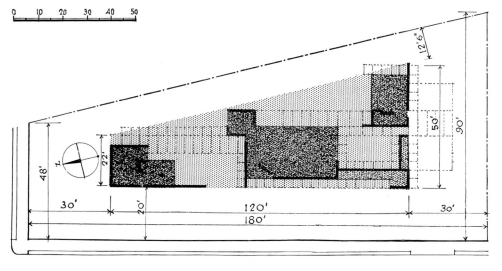

The same 2000 square feet of house "spaced" to incorporate all the land within setback lines has obvious living advantages. The remaining 65% of the lot (white border) is throw-away although it does contribute to community open space. However, compared with European and Mexican methods of handling private and community spaces, it seems infertile, if not provincial.
(See pages 108–109)

Great Neck

Great Neck Colonial with gables.

In considering the plight of suburban houses, tacked to their landscapes with scotch broom and forsythia, it is too easy to blame the architect and builder for their "economies," the antiquated building code for its restrictions, and the enterprising developer for his dollar planning. These conditions can exist only in a culture that is suitable to their growth. The homeowner is not the victim of this culture; he *is* the culture, and aids the process of environmental decay. In every community, to a greater or lesser degree, he slyly contributes by taking part in the neighborhood pressure to conform to practices that are not even in his own interests, but perhaps help him to be more comfortable with his own private phobias.

The streets are quiet in Kensington, but backyard privacy is an achievement. Here it is accomplished by a strong baffle fence of horizontal louvers for side enclosure, and an intricate paving pattern interrupted by water and flowers to focus the attention away from surroundings.

View opposite is seen from a glass-covered trellis directly outside the kitchen. The trellis members were constructed so that screens could be inserted in the openings to avoid the curse of the "screened porch."

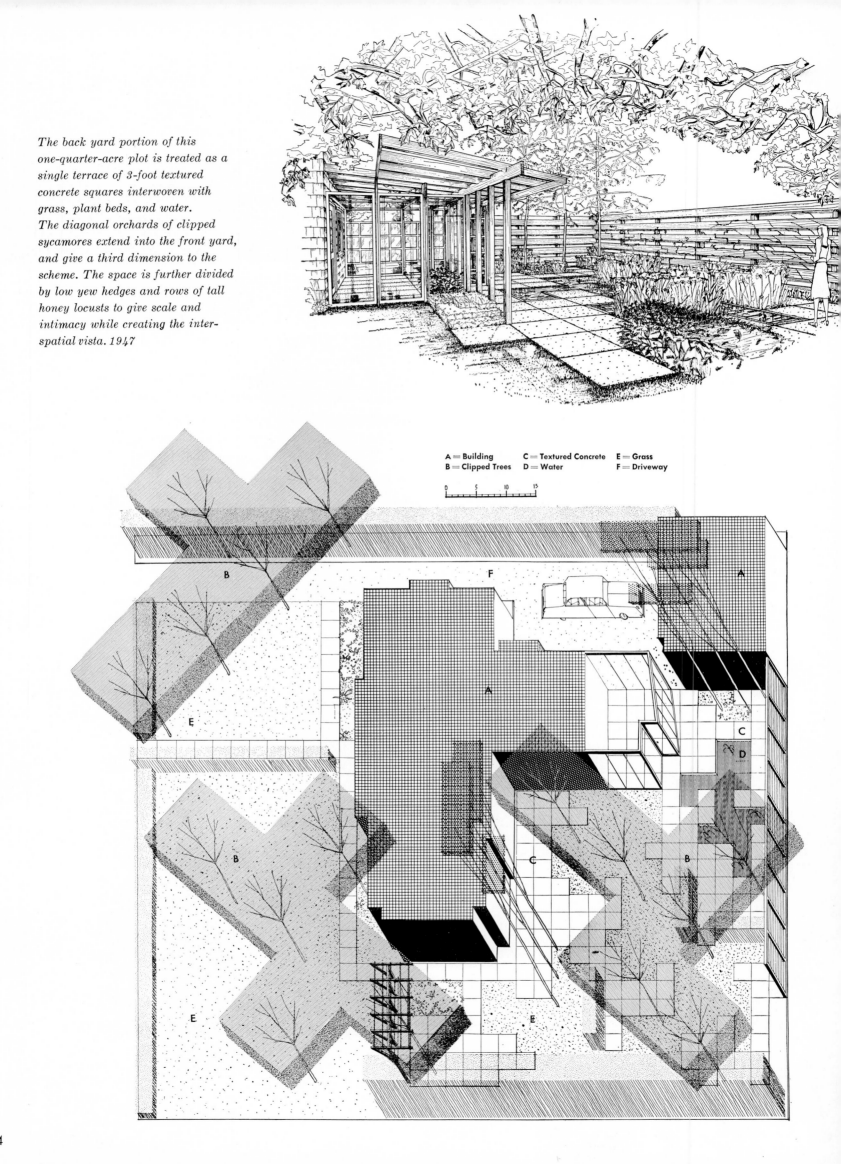

The back yard portion of this one-quarter-acre plot is treated as a single terrace of 3-foot textured concrete squares interwoven with grass, plant beds, and water. The diagonal orchards of clipped sycamores extend into the front yard, and give a third dimension to the scheme. The space is further divided by low yew hedges and rows of tall honey locusts to give scale and intimacy while creating the interspatial vista. 1947

A = Building   C = Textured Concrete   E = Grass
B = Clipped Trees   D = Water   F = Driveway

0   5   10   15

In Kensington, a gate-controlled and police-boothed section of Great Neck, the streets are quiet. Stop signs at alternate corners reduce traffic to an indigenous shuffle. The sidewalk planting, consisting of trees on the curb side and a privet hedge opposite, is maintained by the village to preserve uniformity from the street. Behind this green façade, either by design or decree, most of the lots are $100' \times 100'$, or, as the advertisements read, a "quarter of an acre."

However, a great deal of freedom is permitted in the choice of architectural styles for the houses. Although this particular house is of doubtful vintage, perhaps best described as Great Neck Colonial with gables, the neighboring house on the east is unquestionably a three-storied Simulated-English mansion. Because of its height, it has a better view of this particular back yard than the two-storied, thatched-roofed garage (servant quarters above) that sits on the property line at the south. But the best prospect of the yard, before renovation, was undoubtedly enjoyed by a Great Dane whose run shared the west boundary fence, which was exactly the right height for kibitzing, as Danes are inclined to do.

To create a civilized landscape out of this back yard anarchy, screening became important. The overhead canopy of clipped sycamores in diagonal orchard arrangement baffled the look-down view at strategic points, and created privacy from above as well as a pattern of light and shade; it made a green ceiling, which not only obscured the English Villa and the occupied garage, but somewhat broke the impact of the gables on this house itself. But these sycamores, in addition to a few honey locusts which were used to break the line of the attached garage and give height to the scheme, numbered 27 trees in all on this rather small lot. Furthermore, as I gathered from an hysterical telephone call one spring day, all 27 trees arrived at once, and were standing on the front lawn. Ordinarily, the arrival of plants is no catastrophe, but this time the serenity barrier of the Kensington streets had been broken. Crowds gathered. The neighbors who could not get a better view from their windows, assembled in the street, and in a mood of gay hilarity dubbed the place "Abram's Forest." The name passed, of course, when the trees were in place; no one was conscious of the trees at all, but rather of the space and privacy they created.

Everything was peaceful in Kensington again until a few years later when I did another job in the same community. This time, a neighbor (I think the one in the chateau across the street) became hysterical about what turned out to be an extremely handsome and delicate trellis, but was mistaken for a billboard during construction. I had to go to the Mayor's house with my client to straighten things out. The Mayor was a pleasant man who, during the course of polite conversation, attempted to smooth things over by saying, "These things happen occasionally . . . Why, it was only a few years back that someone on this same street planted sycamore trees . . ."

The detached garage is connected with the house by an 18-inch eggcrate to receive stained glass. The fence, planting, and a stained glass wall under the trellis screens the service, garage doors, basketball practice, and neighboring three-story house. Side door to the garage, between honey locust trees, leads to storage for garden equipment. Paving pattern and pool tend to fuse casually.

Total overhead screening is
accomplished by diagonal orchard
of pleached sycamores which makes
a shaded area for relaxing.
Beyond, the spray jets sparkle in
the sunlight, and flowers enliven
the space. The mosquito screens
and stained glass are in place
under the trellis.

*Night view from the street
entrance to the garden
illuminates the architectural
use of plant forms, and reveals
the sense of space and privacy
achieved in a small area.*

*Look-down view, opposite,
indicates the relation between
the surface pattern of textured
concrete and grass, and the
three-dimensional orchard
pattern of clipped sycamores.*

Miami

Analysis: Here is a typical builder's house in the South Miami landscape. The land is flat—dead flat—broken only by the native pines, tall and dreary in their isolation. Land breezes bring mosquitoes like locusts. The hurricane threat is always present, and the ground surface is a coral bed that needs to be blasted for planting. With it all there is a lush tropical growth, easily moved and re-planted, with the exception of the natural palmetto ground cover.

The usual practice is to clear the land of all vegeta-tion—pines and palmettos alike—plant the tropical version of shrubbery and a coarse native lawn that, under the best conditions, resembles crabgrass; it has the suburban look.

Night view across outdoor dining area to terrace beyond. Lighting makes exotic patterns as it filters through the hanging shelves for aerial plants.

Enclosed entrance court, with parking for seven cars, has a surface of crushed stone identical with the roof. The house façade represents a garden wall, in the total scheme, separating the entrance court from the living areas beyond. The natural palmetto ground cover is retained, and the existing Florida pines form a backdrop contrasting with the man-made landscape.

From the kitchen, the outdoor dining is seen through a beaded bamboo curtain.

Entrance court, as seen from front door, has an indigenous flavor, consciously retained, rather than sacrificed to lawn and shrubbery, to give a sense of continuity with the native landscape. Raised plant bed and planting form an outdoor vestibule protected from parking traffic. Covered passage leading to garage is a convenience in sudden squalls.
Below: entrance façade, like a garden wall, separates the forecourt from private activity beyond.

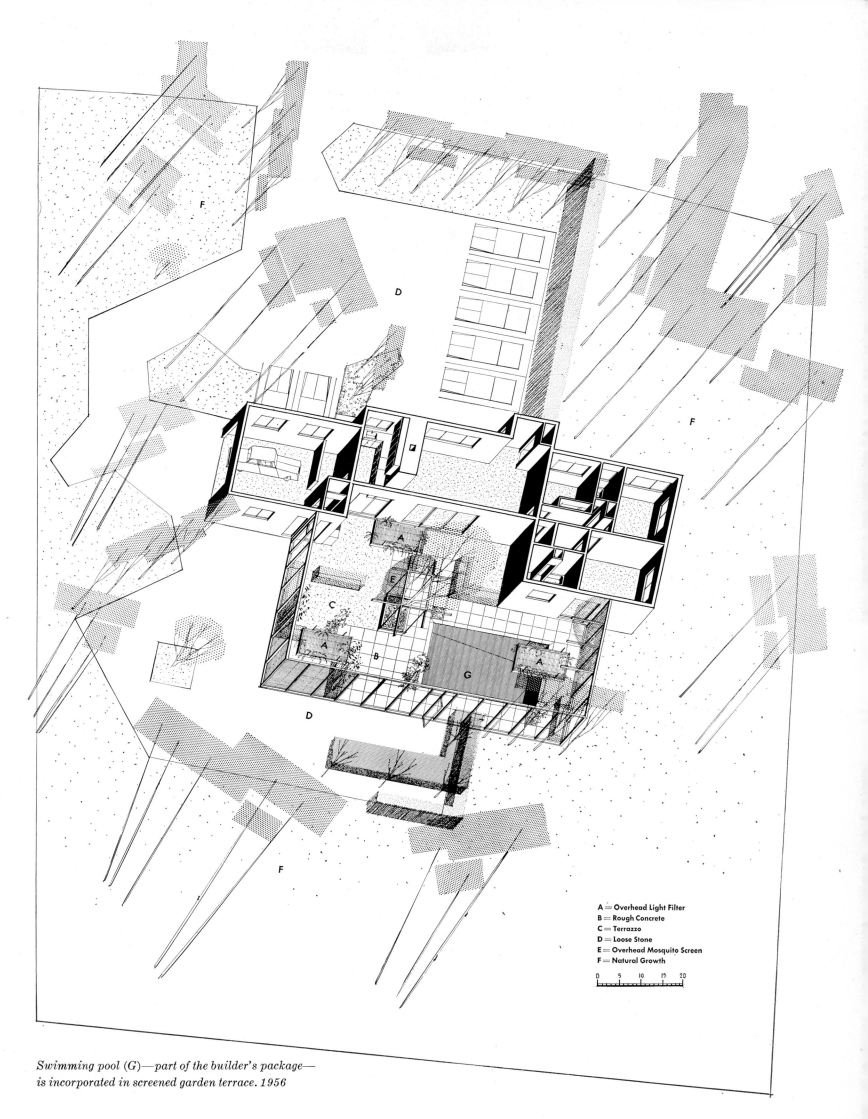

A = Overhead Light Filter
B = Rough Concrete
C = Terrazzo
D = Loose Stone
E = Overhead Mosquito Screen
F = Natural Growth

0   5   10   15   20

Swimming pool (G)—part of the builder's package—
is incorporated in screened garden terrace. 1956

*Right: daytime view from living room
shows the covered portion of terrace in
immediate foreground: this includes
dining area at right, and away-
from-pool sitting area at left
(picture opposite). The active pool
area, middle distance, is paved in
non-skid concrete and separated
from the terrazzo dancing area and
conversational grouping (detail
below) by the encaged Jacaranda
tree, center.*

*Quiet hacienda for nonbathers, in view of the pool,
but protected from splash and sun. Gives the
impression of an interior room.*

*The entire outdoor living area is screened against land-breeze mosquitoes. Jacaranda tree at right breaks the vast expanse;
towering above the roof screens, it gives shade, but is encaged in a screen-well to keep mosquitoes out. Beyond the screen
wall at left is the backdrop of Miami pines. This view across the pool looks toward the sitting area shown opposite.*

A conversational grouping. The suspended egg-crate supports aerial plants and hanging baskets, provides partial shade from the Miami sun during the day, and filters artificial lighting in exotic patterns at night.

Pasadena

*Front entrance: exterior trim is
painted a brownish pink to match the
mahogany-like bark of the guava trees.*

Facing the street, both the house and planting are kept severe, but friendly. The jog in the brick entrance walk, planted with planes of tracery type guava trees and Chinese holly hedges, sets the interspatial feeling of the gardens beyond and provides an extra off street parking for one car. Pittisporum hedge between the existing eucalyptus and the house screens the service while the delicate pattern of a single vine breaks the severity of the façade wall.

The importance and effectiveness of this organic planting is apparent from the "before planting" picture, above.

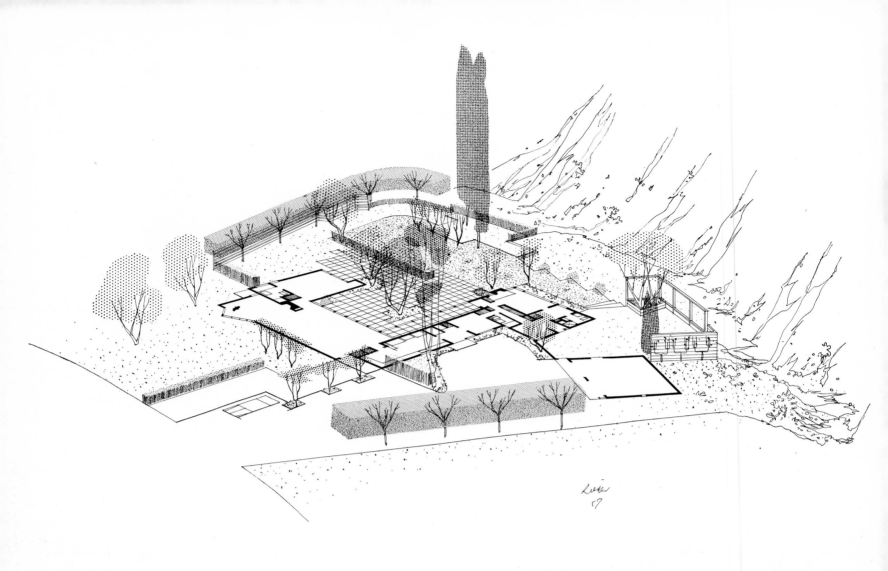

Opposite is the view that greets the visitor on entering the front door. The olive tree (foreground) was moved into the cutout prepared for it in the terrace. Textured paving of court-yard extends through glazed passage leading to owner's suite.

1941: The setting for this Southern California residence was in an already well-developed section. The plot, a truncated wedge, sloped gently and evenly from the curving street to an abrupt drop into an arroyo in the rear. At the edge of this precipice were two magnificent fern trees (Graevillea): beyond, a distant backdrop of snow-capped peaks. This outlook—together with the southwestern exposure—conditioned the major orientation of the whole design. Location of the house across the plot's center was determined by setback restrictions and by the desire for maximum isolation of the owner's suite from the rest of the house.

Working within this reference frame, the design of both the house and the landscape were approached under ideal conditions of collaboration between the architect and landscape architect. The heart of the scheme lies in the complete spatial integration of the exterior and interior. The series of terraces across the entire southwest face of the house, which traditionally would have been segregated and distributed over vast areas, were fused into a single interspatial unit having total immediacy with the house.

Movement in space.

Main terrace, paved with concrete, poured in place between redwood strips, and acid etched to expose the colored aggregate, is perforated by a pattern of beds and indentations to accommodate planting. The terrace, planting, walls, and voids combine to give the space a tactual sense, and a subtle feeling of movement and pattern vibration.

Terrace shape reflects its modular character and flows easily into the lawn. The lawn, in turn, flows past a line of guava trees to an "overlook" terrace, on the precipice, beneath fern trees. A wide ramp, lined with pleached sycamores, returns to the main terrace.

1   At the front entrance, the planting was completed by a high hedge to screen service area, low hedges to emphasize direction of walk and separate walk from parking.

2   Along bedroom, projecting hedge diverts circulation away from bedroom window, and low, saucer-type plants direct the interest toward sun patio.

3   At difficult chimney spot, planting complements the line and mass of the building, and relates it to the landscape.

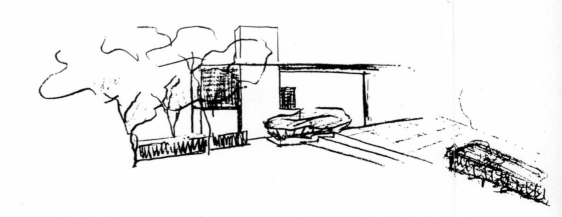

4 *With existing live oak tree, this bedroom requires only a single, low specimen at corner of building. Terrace is between house and foreground hedge.*

Still under construction at the beginning of World War II, the landscape was completed by mail, so to speak. The owner sent snapshots of areas where the intention was not clearly understood, and I returned overlay sketches describing the size, form, and name of plants to be used. Photographs after completion demonstrate how well and faithfully the owner followed these sketches in the final execution.

5 *Woven fence, insufficient in itself to obscure neighboring house, was supplemented by clipped sycamore trees. View below shows bedroom terrace (4) and woven fence (5) with planting completed.*

At the time that the resistance labeled "modern" architecture as cold and impersonal, this contemporary design in California achieved the warmth of early Spanish architecture—a form much imitated by the opponents of contemporary.

At the extreme western corner, in the angle formed by the back of the garage and the edge of the arroyo, is a private patio off the owners suite; it is enclosed by a transparent glass screen to capture the sun and exclude the wind, and is focused on the snow-capped peaks.

South Orange

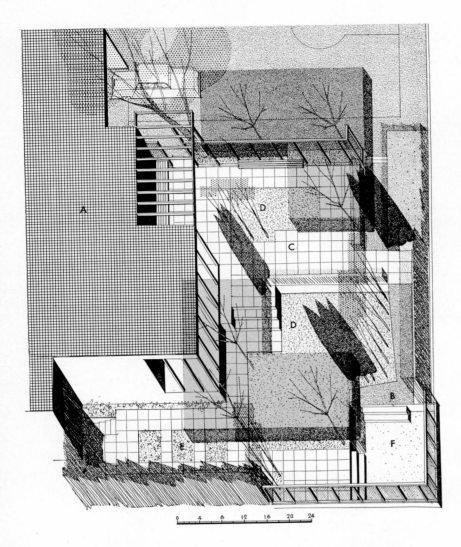

0 4 8 12 16 20 24

A-House   **B-Blacktop**   **C-Flagstone**
D-Grass   **E-Beds**   **F-Pebbles**

Originally a nondescript back yard, this landscape just happened to be left over after building a house which, to be sure, satisfied all restrictions and code requirements. The mixture of neighboring buildings can best be described as architecturally "tossed," each with the usual shrubbery dressing and contour, which somehow never adds up to either privacy or usefulness. The off-living portion of this particular yard was rendered useless by a four-foot-in-fifty diagonal slope to the corner of the property. In fact, the only useable space was a paved garage court at the rear which resulted from the owner's objection to having garage doors face the street, and only incidentally made an excellent play surface for the children. The lack of any "liveable" outdoor space for adults led to the addition of a screened porch which, in turn, acquired a rather expensive awning as a protection against the west sun. Accomplishing all these needs with thoughtful landscaping was not considered until the other ventures had proved themselves dull and inadequate. The optimistic ingredient was a warmhearted, gregarious, and integrated family unit that deserved no less than to have these qualities expressed in their surroundings. 1954

Reconstruction of diagonal slope into terrace levels makes every square inch of land useable. Organic planting scheme gives privacy, shade, and optimum awareness of space. Pattern of grass and paving reflects the circulation. No attempt is made at total screening or segregation of areas, but rather a sense of privacy and separation of activity, as shown opposite. The living area is separated from the motor-play court and service by a wood frame strung vertically with white nylon cord and a delicate, summer blooming vine—Clematis henryi.

Approach to garden from play space is baffled by low azalea hedge. Conversational
group on terrace is left undisturbed, but visible through flowering cherry trees. Existing
screened porch is seen through tracery of white birch clumps, and partly baffled by
vertical hedge of cryptomeria at steps leading to lower level.

From door of screened porch one looks back to the lounging terrace.
Grass is used as a carpet in the paving, and the motor-play court
is visible but separated by nylon screen.

Children gather in anticipation of an afternoon picnic. The gravel-surfaced picnicking area, at lowest level (determined by existing tree), communicates with the play court by ramp, and with screened porch by flagstone walk. Before picture shows previous unuseable slope.

When the family decides to dine outdoors at table, the children are always at hand in the play court. Dining area is central to play court, screened porch, kitchen, and lounging area. Before picture shows a few of the revisions: notably, trellis breaks the west sun, and makes screened porch seem to belong.

West Orange

In a typical New Jersey suburb, with its eternal problems of privacy, this little garden serves as an entrance court; the house architect had arranged the main entrance at the rear to leave the front view uninterrupted from the living room. The garden communicates with the kitchen and growing area as well as the entrance, and provides an all-purpose outdoor space remarkable for its relaxed and casual uses. The space is man-made since there were no natural advantages to draw upon. The land sloped upward to an open field—nondescript, except for a vintage mansion of menacing proportions—neighbors, on either side, as usual.

The garden, graded into two distinct levels to take advantage of the slope and achieve maximum useable areas, is screened from the more dominant elements of its surroundings. Planting, entirely brought in, and light-feeling construction conspire to give another-world quality while partly accepting the immediate environment.

1952

Overhead trellis has dual purpose of structural bracing and decorative patterns—repeated in shadows on the ground. The blacktop surface, broken by occasional lozenges of grass, gives a sense of fluidity to an otherwise stabile-type construction, while diagonal bracing of side frames permits long, uninterrupted spans, and translucent panels insure privacy where needed.

Below: main entrance to both house and garden is seen through frame opening and planting.

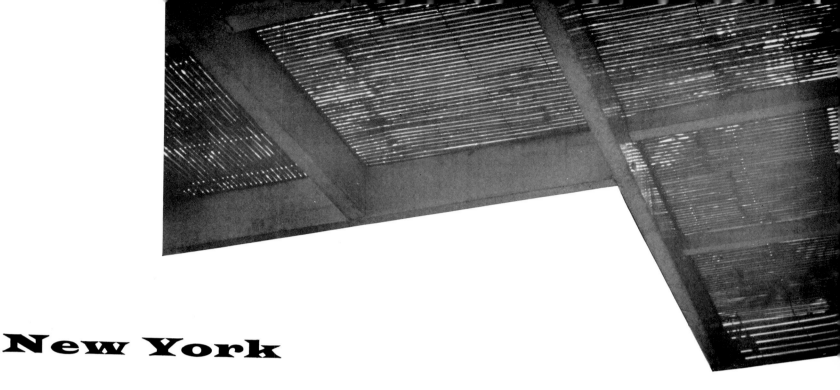

New York

It is a common delusion, particularly American, I believe, that space in itself solves problems. If a man has a fifty foot lot, he wants a hundred; if he has a hundred, he wants an acre; if he has an acre, he wants ten. And yet, the man with acreage has the same problems as the man with the fifty foot lot—they are simply distributed over more territory, and therefore less apparent to him; when he moves from the intolerable city, he takes his problems with him creating the rural and suburban slum; when he moves into the wilderness, he creates a dust bowl.

In *The Treasure of Sierra Madre*, there is a scene where, high in the mountains and far from civilization, the old man astounds his less dedicated companions by insisting that they refill the mine, where they have dug gold, before returning to civilization—the point being that, as in any organism, nature's wounds must be mended, no matter where they happen. This is hardly less true for man's large scale plundering of nature which we call a city; the imbalance is only more grotesque, the problem more apparent.

I do not think the wound will be healed by back yard gardens for brownstone houses. The rebalance must be integral with the concept of a city; a band-aid of foliage cannot be applied after the plunder is complete—as we attempt to do in our suburbs. But the oasis is important. It is especially important if it implies the benefits of space discipline rather than expansion and spoiling. For there still are benefits of a culture that can be realized only within the high density population of a metropolis.

1958

Privacy, the keynote to this city garden, is accomplished by overhead trellis—perforated to allow columnar ginkgo trees to project through.

Conditions for growing plants in
midtown Manhattan are so difficult
that the architectural part of the garden
is emphasized here. Except for columnar
ginkgoes, all plants are in special
containers for easy replacement. These
intimate views show the hanging pan
of begonias foiled against sapling
fence and translucent panels while it is
(opposite) silhouetted dramatically
against the superstructure. Water lilies
and other aquatics are in raised
galvanized pan, and potted ivy hangs
from the trellis.

The ground surface is a transition from white asphalt tile (interior) to white marble paving set in concrete (middle ground) to white marble chips (foreground). Cellar stairway, necessary access to storage, is relieved by decorative grille railing and reduced in importance by introduction of raised pool pan of similar proportions.

Transformation in white: another New York City back yard, designed in collaboration with the owner-architect, reflects the simplicity and sophistication possible to achieve from almost sordid beginnings. Objectionable elements are "handled" rather than attempting total obliteration in so small an area. The all-white surfaces give the impression of purity in design which belies the inherent difficulties overcome in developing this very liveable environment.

The side walls, necessarily high for privacy, make transition from brick to vertical wood siding. The outline is broken with window-like perforations to avoid monotony and relieve constriction. Night view shows lighting, and water activated by spray jets. 1956

East Meadows

In a community of open space, but no privacy, the two photographs above—taken from a screened terrace—show levels and planting working together to create a sense of privacy under difficult conditions. The sapling fence (upper right) testifies to previous attempts at enclosure along property line.

This Long Island project posed two of the most difficult problems in the work of a landscape architect: privacy and the screened porch. With ample dimension on all sides, it was impossible to find a square foot unexposed to a neighboring picture window. Although privacy was wished for as much by the neighbors as by my clients, sporadic attempts at screening with sapling fences proved ineffective, and total screening with plants would have consumed most of the useable space. I suggested raising the ground along the border of the property by two step-back retaining walls to gain the additional height before screening began. The effect would be that of a sunken garden, with a degree of privacy gained by keeping the screen planting high. In this way, smaller plants could be used, and the difference in price would justify the cost of wall building and bringing in fill.

The average "screened porch" I find as indefensible and archaic as a "parlor," but since protection against insects was important in this locality, I suggested a kind of screened trellis or loggia—raised in level to block passage from the street to the inner garden—that communicated with both the dining room and the garden. 1956

*Step-back retaining walls provide a garden walk and seating space
around central "sunken" area. Picnicking-barbecue area (opposite)
communicates with kitchen and looks back over sunken area through
the tracery of birch trees which emphasize the horizontal levels.*

Raised screened terrace separates the garden from the street. Thin white vertical lines are nylon cord strung to support vines and to reinforce screening from the street.

Mineola

In this Long Island builder's community, privacy and enclosure are suggested by a canopy of wisteria suspended on wire rope between a central steel mast and wood frame. Complete obliteration of the surroundings is not attempted.

Outdoor dining, (left) as seen from the kitchen stoop, is separated from the lounging space (below) by translucent, plastic-impregnated wire mesh screen in 3- by 3-feet wood frames.

1950. This one had all the problems: a corner lot that exposed the house to the street on two sides, a garage that came between the house and the only possible garden area—with access to it from either the front door or from the kitchen, off a tiny platform three feet above ground level; from either approach, it was necessary to circumvent the garage to get to the garden. The house next door also had a kitchen, windows facing, at a distance of eighteen feet so that neighborly conversations over fried eggs were possible. Another neighbor had a perfect view into the potential garden from a much-used deck over his garage. The rest was street—the street of a typical builder's development—with a jungle of telephone poles, electric wires, and sidewalk lamps as flora—making the children at play seem, somehow, less than fauna.

I refused this job three times. Like the champion swearer, who became so flabbergasted he could think of nothing to say, I could think of nothing to do with it. Then the owners, a charming couple who had dreamed of having a garden all through the privations of World War II, threw down a most ingenuous challenge. They told me that they realized it was an impossible situation, but (they had decided) that if anyone could do anything with it, I could. This is the kind of flattery that no self respecting ego can resist. So, like Caesar with the crown, I finally accepted—with the cautious stipulation that the project would be completed in one season; I did not think it possible to sustain the proper interest for a five year plan.

I knew this had to be a tour de force. I knew it had to be "done," and the thought momentarily disrupted my theory of just "not preventing" things from happening. But, I discovered, the human jungle is only hostile to aspiration in the same degree as the natural one; both require control and discipline, and particularly, a frame of reference for human awareness. In the long run, this is survival.

My first thought was of privacy—privacy in all dimensions, and all encompassing: it led to the idea of a structural mast with wire rope suspended overhead like a web, with the ends anchored in the ground for stability. From here, everything clicked into place. The enclosing frame structure took the sag out of the wire rope which, in turn, stabilized the frame, and supported wisteria vines that hung like a great tree, giving privacy and shelter over head. A pattern of translucent and open squares in the frame permitted light and air, but baffled the neighbors' view from the sides; recessing the frame slightly provided a planting space between it and the property line so that branches could protrude into the garden through the openings and silhouette against the translucent panels from behind while presenting a "friendly" face to the neighbors. And so on, to the last detail.

But it is a rough haul from conception to the accomplished fact in the human jungle. In this instance, the natives were particularly restless, but they followed a more or less stereotyped pattern:

First, a show of friendly cooperation. In order to have a frame enclosure beyond the building setback line, the owner had to petition and get signatures of all neighbors within a specified distance. But the signatures were no problem. Approached individually, all signed with proper felicitation; everyone wants to be thought well of, and what is a partly open frame between neighbors?

Followed by suspicion and resentment. Quite likely, some of the neighbors visualized a nine foot frame as about waist high. In any event, there was the dramatic moment when nine feet actually became nine feet. Why? That was the question. Could it be that these people disliked their neighbors? Or were they just snobs? At this point, the reaction was collective rather than individual, and went underground. The women said little things about who thought they were better than whom, and the men scurried about checking property lines against encroachment.

Next, envy. This stage was relatively pleasant. As the garden began to take shape, mutual benefits became evident. Fully grown plants were brought in, facing the neighboring properties. The frame could hardly be seen. But who did these people think they were? Rockefeller? "They would never get their money out of it."

Then, the kill. The garden had just been completed when Long Island decided to have a hurricane. Everyone had *said* those frames would never stand up, and now it seemed that the whole community gathered in the street to watch them blow down. The festivities were brief, however. The wind carried with it identifiable items of garden bric-a-brac—sections of picket fence, a wheelbarrow, an unplanted shrub—and, one by one, the spectators ran home to secure their own moorings. The controversial frame did pretty well. The openings permitted the wind to find its way, and the wire rope held it steady. It came through without a scratch.

Finally, acceptance. About a year later, in the springtime, the owners decided to give a garden party for the neighbors. The canopy of wisteria was in bloom, the translucent panels in the frame made a perfect background for the women's dresses, and good manners were rampant. It was quite a civilized gathering—with just a tinge of possessiveness toward the garden "right next door." I got the impression that if, at that moment, someone from another neighborhood had wandered past, and sneered, he would have been frozen to the telephone wires with icy glances.

A-Blacktop B-Brick C-Pachysandra D-Beds E-Grass F-Mast G-House H-Garage

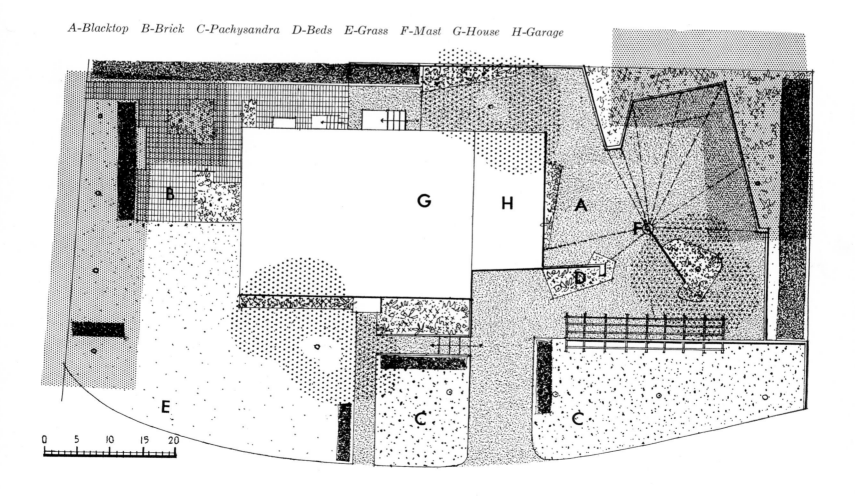

The original brick stoop, connecting kitchen with outdoor dining, is screened from the neighbor's kitchen by translucent sunray glass in trellis frame. Screen directs circulation toward garden proper. Dining area is separated from conversational grouping (right) by projecting frame wall and planting to avoid interruption of either activity by circulation.

Privacy is suggested rather than made absolute.

A down shot from deck over the garage shows a garden at work and people at play. The average back yard becomes sculpture —not in the ordinary sense of an object to be looked at—but sculpture that is large enough and perforated enough to walk through, open enough to present no barrier to movement, and broken enough to guide the experience . . . a sense of rhythm and a sense of being within something while still out of doors.

Right: *a quiet corner twenty feet from the sidewalk.*
Middle: *privacy in the builder's jungle.*
Lower right: *garden entrance from the street
showing cantilever trellis.*

Fusion – a step

toward integration

Ridgewood

In *The Last Puritan*, Santayana points out that his hero is so young he does not yet realize everything is wrong with the world—everything from the leaky faucet to affairs of state. And, believe me, I have no compulsion to set it right. I do things for my own comfort. And one of the things that makes a landscape consultant uncomfortable is continually having to patch up the mistakes of others—the developer, the builder, the architect, and the owner.

By the time I am called in, the situation is epidemic. The money is all spent. The foundation is three feet out of the ground. The service is on the wrong side of the house. There is no access to the living room from outdoors. A concrete patio, complete with barbecue, is in progress. The lot has been cleared of vegetation. The land is eroding. Mud is being tracked on the new rug. And I am expected to do something exciting and interesting that will make it all seem right as rain.

Unfortunately, the situation *can* be helped by good landscaping. Unfortunately, because landscaping then becomes just another crutch to lean on, and a rather expensive crutch, at that, since to correct these little mistakes properly will average about fifteen percent of the cost of the house. Even so, the results can never be comparable, in living value, to a thorough integration from the beginning.

Realizing this, and having been subjected to the discomfort of patchwork long enough, the day finally came when a client showed me a set of house plans that seemed to epitomize every fault of ingrown architecture. While it was large and expensive, it was possessed by every cliché, from ribbon windows in the semi-circular bays, to gurgling fountains in the foyer, and it communicated about as much with the site as a roller skating rink. When I pointed out some of the difficulties in "landscaping" such a house, the client said, "What do you care about the house? You can trellis the hell out of it when it's finished."

I am not denying that this is a currently one-hundred-percent American attitude. It was just enough so to make me take stock of the patch-work situation. At the top is the arbitrary subdivision of the land that cuts the cloth, so to speak, for its own purpose. Then, obsolete restrictions are applied which prevent its use except in a preconceived pattern. A house, more often than not designed in an intellectual vacuum, is added. And finally the client with a naïve, but devastating, conditioned attitude really believes that everything can be set right with a little "landscaping."

At this point, I decided it would at least be one step forward, and throw the patchwork into better perspective, to design the house as part of the landscape rather than permit it to be imposed on the site. I had no particular desire to take on domestic architecture in the ordinary sense. Polite wrangling over whether to have a Formica or a linoleum top, to the exclusion of concept, is not my idea of either comfort or architecture. It was more in the nature of self defense, and it seemed like more fun to make one's own mistakes than to rectify the mistakes of others.

I think the experiment illustrates both the spatial and esthetic increment of the fusion. The walls become garden walls instead of barriers. The landscape is of the house instead of attached to it, and the space is one. I wonder what it would be like, in a community sense, to reach those little men who slice the land before they slice it?

Guest house and hearth

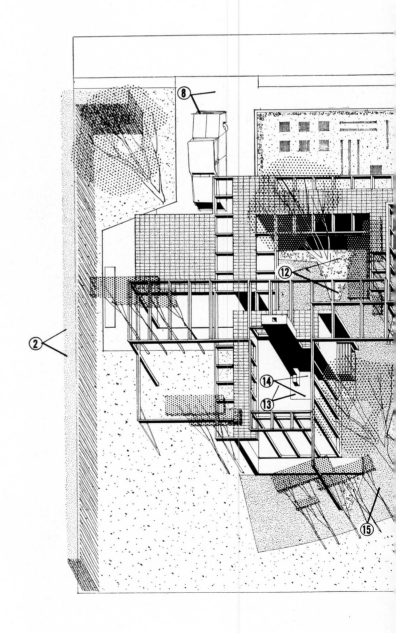

Bedroom garden   **Bed and dressing room**   **Fireplace**   **Living room from main terrace**

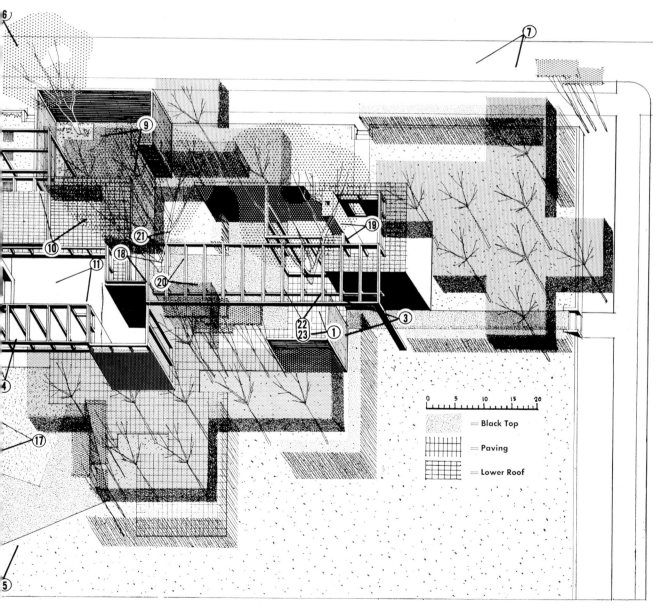

| 0 | 5 | 10 | 15 | 20 |

▦ = Black Top

▦ = Paving

▦ = Lower Roof

The layout of a living complex for three adults comprises a guest house, main house, and studio, interspersed with gardens. Open spaces are made integral with the enclosed. (See lot diagram comparisons page 51). 1952

Numbers refer to photographs that follow.

"Official" front entrance through garden court.

For a long time I had watched, with bird-like curiosity, clients wringing their hands and hovering just above nervous collapse. I often asked myself, "Why don't they relax?" Now I know. And in my humbled opinion, anyone who builds is a hero. The reason is partly financial, of course, but I rather think that the real cause is to be found elsewhere. For if one were dead set against being a hero, and still wished to build, the simplest approach would not be to have a lot of money, but to appoint the proper committee to design the building, and thereby avoid all friction. There would certainly be no friction between a committee composed of the local building inspector, a finance company, a builder who employs an architect (rather than vice versa), and two or three of the prospective neighbors. The only thing that could be simpler is buying the house that the same committee has built down the street.

My own aims were slightly different. Practically, it had to be a house for three adults—with complete individual privacy to avoid conflict in work, entertainment, and personality, and yet arranged to become an effective community unit for family activity when the occasion or inclination demanded. It should slide easily from individual to group function.

In the beginning, I was not at all sure what architectural form such requirements would assume. Although I had toyed with the idea before, the actual form did not evolve until I had acquired a lot which had remained empty because of its obvious difficulties. It was a corner lot with 48 feet frontage on the main street, which splayed to 90 feet at the rear, and 180 feet deep along a side street (see page 51). As the setback restrictions stood, the actual building area was 12 feet fronting the main street, splaying to 40 feet at the rear, and 120 feet deep along the side street. After probing the building inspector's office, I discovered that if the "official" front entrance could be devised to fit on the 12-foot side, an extra 10 feet would be allowed on the side street, making a total of 22 feet, splaying to 50 feet by 120 feet deep.

At the time, I found the challenge of fitting all requirements of the individual and collective indoor-outdoor living complex on to this lot a fascinating project to study. It developed into a composite house of three

Fireplace detail, main house.

complete buildings—one for each individual—architecturally unified by the spaces between. Its flexibility in layout permit the three units to be used as (1) a main house, (2) studio, and (3) guest house—as I have shown it here. The result was a tiny village.

I decided to go at the construction as you might a painting or a piece of sculpture. I set up the basic armature of walls, and roofs, and open spaces to establish their relationships, but left it free in detail to allow for improvisation. In that way it would never be "finished," but constantly evolving from one stage to the next—a metamorphosis such as we find, commonly, in nature.

The idea sat on the local New Jersey cerebellum like hair that comes with the hat. Everyone in Ridgewood knows what a house is. The building inspector drew one for me, gratuitously, the day I applied for a building permit, and showed me just how to place it on the lot.

Without being in the least hypersensitive, I could foresee difficulty, and decided to ask a local architect, familiar with the code requirements, to check the plans and specifications against violations to prevent any tie-up during construction. After inquiries of the inspector's office and what I judged, from his tone, to be more or less "influential" neighbors, he said that the feelings against the house ran so high that he doubted I would ever get it built. In any event, he could not risk his own business by having anything to do with it.

If I had not been serious before, I was now, and decided to go it alone. The building inspector turned out to be just another guy trying to hold down a job, and gave me remarkably little trouble, except when public spirited citizens reported what they thought to be violations. Actually, I took great pains not to violate any codes. I followed them to the letter, and made them work for me—much to the inspector's dismay. For instance, in addition to the simple device of calling one door the front entrance, instead of another, and thereby gaining ten feet of building space along the broad side of the property, I gained privacy where no walls were permitted—even within the building setback line—by making them storage and utility walls, instead of free standing—thereby coming within the law again.

Building codes are intended to protect the prospective home owner from faulty or unsafe construction. They have no esthetic function, I am happy to say, and since all the objections turned out to be esthetic rather than structural, they dwindled to a small gurgle in the inspector's throat and passed away.

It was a difficult experience for Ridgewood. While the citizenry is conservative, it is well bred. Second looks are unthinkable. And here it was confronted with something that demanded attention, perhaps reprisal, but exactly how that could be done, in a dignified manner, was a problem. The mayor made several unofficial visits during construction, but apparently found nothing amiss. The inspector had lost his spirit entirely, and just wanted to get through with the job. The house obviously had ideas and certain living advantages, but if they were admitted, how could one justify one's own?

From my point of view, it was a happy house. From the moment it was enclosed, something happened acoustically that made voices sound beautiful. It had an earthy quality that made people look and act like characters in a Chekhov play; artificial poses were impossible. But especially, it had its own moods—the moods of nature. Sunlight falls in the right places, and it is capable of dramatic change with the occasion, with the season, and with the time of day. It defies photography because it is only partly optic, and always in sequence—building to a total impression rather than single "effects." I have never seen it twice alike, and in a community of people it retains an awareness of the most Unprejudiced Being of all.

It must have been two or three years later, during a consultation in Connecticut, when mortal resistance showed itself again. At a respect-provoking fee, I had just staked out revisions on a "problem" landscape inherited from a builder's dilemma, and the clients were immensely pleased with the results. At lunch, the conversation ran high and fast, and finally settled down to the "do you know" phase, and a truly delicious moment. It turned out that the wife was formerly from Ridgewood, and the town came up for scrutiny. "Have you seen that new monstrosity down by the high-school?" she asked, gaily. Without the slightest hesitation, I responded, "Oh, yes. That's my house."

Right: studio, from the street, is lighted by clerestory dome. Wood grille slot can be seen through from inside, but not from street.

Below: street façade of main house is storage and utility wall—behind, a walled bedroom garden.

Opposite: service entrance is flanked by a cut-flower-vegetable-and-fruit garden, directly between sidewalk and house, and a kitchen garden behind bamboo screen.

8

9

Above: from the kitchen garden, one already has the feeling of being inside. Bamboo screens are mocked up to test their sufficiency as screening. Rope trick is for supporting grape vines.

Opposite: the dining space becomes part of the kitchen garden. Block wall extends beyond house with glass channeled into it, giving continuity to house and garden.

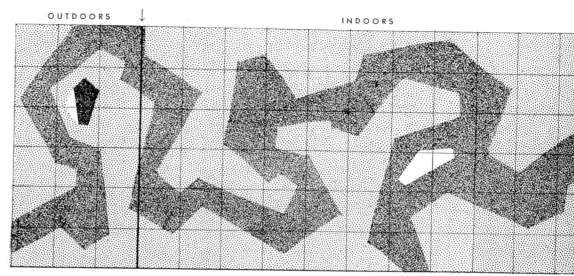

OUTDOORS ↓ INDOORS

Mosaic mural, "River of Hospitality" design, is to be applied to wall below.

*From dining space, the view
across living room to main terrace.*

11

12

*A private, walled garden off the main house bed and dressing rooms
communicates with the main terrace (right) and guest house.*

Down shot of the main, all-purpose terrace shows interlocking forms of grass and blacktop in combination with concrete walk and plant forms. This terrace is equally accessible from the main house and guest house.

14

From the guest house hearth, the view across terrace to main house. Hearth extends outdoors becoming plant box.

Opposite: existing wild cherry tree frames the hearth-extended plant box and seat niche, main house walled bedroom garden beyond.

Lighting becomes an integral part of this indoor-outdoor design. Open block grille of guest house fireplace, illuminated from behind, penetrates the glass wall between interior and main terrace, and divides the hearth-extended plant pocket from integral garden seat. At left, solid house wall, extended, forms back of garden seat and continues the enclosure of walled bedroom garden of main house.

19

Opposite: view from main house entrance across court entrance to studio (extreme left). Occasionally twisted bamboo sections, suspended from frame, give a "falling leaves" pattern, and the tree-in-trellis canopy gives a sense of enclosure.

Above: from studio hearth across court to main house entrance.

View diagonally across court into studio. Interior-exterior wall from wood grille is slated for future mural. Note continuous lighting cove, outdoor painting, and trellis lantern (center).

Entrance to the entrance court. "Falling Leaves" bamboo between two wood columns becomes a light diffuser at night. Fountain spray cools the summer air.
Nylon cord etches subtle division between studio and main court. Screen-covered wood grille acts as screen door.
Note paper painting screen of balsa wood and translucent, colored paper in studio window. Cast block in table frames recalls paving at entrance.

21

Day and night. Identical views looking into studio living space. Exterior-
interior wall, from wood grille, to be one continuous mural. Existing linden
tree pierces overhead trellis, flowers limited to hanging basket and
naturalized bulbs, jet spray cools atmosphere—creates sound.

22

23

Baltimore

My friend and master, Antonin Raymond, used to say of clients (inevitably as Polonius), "If they spend fifty thousand, they will do something bad; if they spend a hundred thousand, it will be a masterpiece of vulgarity." I have found that this inevitable pronouncement of the embittered master is not inevitably true—although it is true frequently enough, in communities that relish the display of wealth, to give pause. For my own part, I like rich people. They have the irresistible appeal of needing rescue more than anyone because they are in a position to carry projects to their logical conclusions.

I first visited Baltimore, like the man who came to dinner, for a brief consultation—a consultation specifically restricted to advice about which trees should be cut down to accommodate a new house, and improve the property generally. As in so many top level conferences, nothing else should be considered. I could not help but notice, however, that the site on which the trees were located—a one and a half acre hillside lot—dropped fifty feet in two hundred. And I could see that, by the time 5,000-square feet of a one-level house were placed on such a slope (twenty five percent), with all the grading, driveways, and services called for, there would not be many trees left to worry about.

The property was heavily wooded with tall oaks and magnificent beeches, but otherwise suburbanly undistinguished. On the top side, it was bordered by a typical Baltimore alley, with Charles Addams houses descending, drably. On either side, the neighboring houses were an unidentifiable mixture of styles and constructions: to the north, a mildly pleasant, but inconsequential, view across the valley to more houses, and directly below, a main traffic artery which seemed to be the chief attraction because it lead so quickly to downtown Baltimore.

House plans devised by the original architect clearly stated a series of rigid demands, posed by the owners—the most astonishing of which was that the entire house should be on one level, regardless of its size or the contour of the land. This was complicated by another mandatory requirement—that the layout should be so arranged that the children's portion could be supervised by the servants or the parents, but that the responsibility should never conflict or become open to dispute. At least, it should

not deteriorate to the untenable situation of the maid supervising the mistress supervising the children. All this indicated an enormous house which, since the landscape was now being considered only as an afterthought, would inevitably bulge, like a Christmas turkey, over the land.

Outdoor requirements were more nebulous (and not discussed at the first meeting which was restricted to "trees"). The husband was of the "just make it beautiful" school of thought. "I have hayfever, and will stay indoors with the air-conditioning, anyway." He was against a swimming pool from the beginning. The wife thought she would like a pool, but was not quite sure because she "would never forgive herself if anything happened to a child. . . ." (We got the pool.)

One thing was certain—any amount of ground modeling, with or without considering the trees, would be possible since the owner was in the construction business. Heavy and light equipment, with skilled operators, would be on the job at all times—an almost unheard of convenience, as landscape work goes. I was slightly mystified by an even stranger condition: if I should take the job, I was not to know the cost of anything, great or small—apparently so that my judgment would be free to make the proper selections rather than effect economies or acquire costly possessions. I think this also had something to do with my alleged "common touch" which was not to be lost under any circumstances.

I was not sure, at this point, that I would accept the job, even under these semiattractive conditions; at the time of our next meeting, in Ridgewood, I was certain that I would not. The original architect had been discharged for "unavailability," and a local one appointed, "tentatively," to execute the plans of the first. This is never an ideal situation, and it was even less so in this instance because the new architect, openly unsympathetic, was understandably bewildered as to how to proceed with another's incomplete sketches. The owners, feeling that they had been put through the paces and had lost precious time, were adamant about getting started, and were unitedly determined to use the sketches they had paid for no matter who they would have to get to execute them. My own cautioning met with the now

famous cry, "What do you care about the building? You can trellis the hell out of it when it's finished."

I had made up my mind to have nothing to do with the job under these circumstances, but since the three of them had driven all the way to Ridgewood for consultation on an insufferable August day, and had the good grace not once to mention the weather, I decided to throw down a challenge. I suggested that, instead of making a hasty decision, if they would grant me one week end's time, I would come back to Baltimore, and, working night and day on the spot, would produce a new scheme including both house and landscape that would fit the ground without disturbing a single tree, and without changing any of the established house requirements. I had no idea how this could possibly be done, but I did know that the effort would be more rewarding, and that the method would save time in the long run, and that the results would be infinitely superior as compared to the struggle of one architect to read another one's mind.

The local, "tentative," architect agreed that this approach was somewhat out of his line, but offered to assist in any way possible in making drawings or getting them approved by the building inspector. I immediately checked with the original architect in New York to clear any ethical questions that might still be involved, and with his blessings, I proceeded to Baltimore the next week end to take charge.

It was a happy experience. The young couple were intelligent and cooperative, and, on reflection, extremely appreciative for having been "saved." They recognized this as a new experience, and rather than maintaining a conventional pose of owner-telling-the-architect, they asked me what their attitude should be—whether they should go on a vacation and let me alone, for instance. My instinctive reaction to this was that it would be the worst kind of vacuum to work in; I would almost rather have a nagging client. I, too, recognized this as a unique experience, and explained to them what I hoped to accomplish, and how it could best be done. I wanted them actively engaged in the concept so that they would understand what was going on each step of the way.

And here is a slight paradox: it is much easier to do something for clients before they realize it fully, and yet their presence is quite as necessary as the site itself to act as a two-way sounding board. I think the reason is partly that clients, being untrained, tend to jump immediately to finished surfaces, and are inclined to be impatient with concepts until they become a reality. Partly, also, is the fact that an effective concept is not likely to be arrived at by a committee. On the other hand, personal arrogance on the part of the designer is fatal. It is not so much a question of what *I* will do to a given site or with a client's problem, as what the combination of site and problem will do to *me*.

There is a wonderful period in the formation of any design when you are working alone—within these limits. At this time, the direction is established, and what I like to call the armature—from which all parts fall into place. This is the essence which embraces the yet unformed detail, and still permits the detail to form naturally. It is not entirely a personal thing because it is conditioned by the site and must anticipate the feelings of everyone concerned. In this instance, I knew the concept would have to be strong—strong enough to shine through those inevitable days of reckoning with volatile tastes, sidewalk critics, unaccustomed technicians, unskilled labor, and grey flannel envy.

My thoughts on the basic concept were, first, it should begin with the land, and the land should be sculpture—a bas-relief creating level areas at the base of trees with the trees left undisturbed. I plotted all the trees on a contour map and studied the myriad possibilities for making levels—intervening, overlapping, projecting levels—with not disturbing trees as the basic discipline. I selected one level large enough to take the house, and an existing valley into which the pool could be tortured. The landscape problem, from then on, was a question of simplifying and integrating the various levels within a system of circulation.

The house turned out to be not quite so formidable a problem as it first appeared. It fell neatly into three parts: (1) the master's, with bedroom-study and living-dining space, off the pool terraces; (2) the children's, comprising three sleeping cubicles—each with its garden access—and a common playroom communicating with a private play yard; and (3) the service, which included the kitchen and utility room—connecting with the delivery entrance from the alley above—and two servants' rooms, one of which might double as an occasional guest room.

The separation of these three parts is not as actual as it may sound, for each is thoroughly interrelated, but the parts are defined enough, architecturally, to break the enormity of the house as it sits on the land. The atrium, brought into the center, brings with it a sense of the landscape continuing through the house, and the interior passageways, bordering the atrium on two sides, directly communicate with the outdoors.

We did the landscape first—maintaining the strictest discipline about storing and transporting building materials so they would not interfere. While still waiting for the building permit (I was assured there could be no mishap), we poured the floor slab of the house, built the retaining walls which established the ground forms, even did some of the planting—everything but the superstructure of the house and the swimming pool. The pool was still in controversy, and I did not know for sure which way it would go. I devised a shape to follow the land contour with the least excavation and to fit between existing trees, taking the precaution that it would be a fine addition, if built, complimenting the terrace, or a pleasant natural valley if it were not.

At this stage, one got an unobstructed bird's-eye view from the alley above. The forms had begun to emerge, and it had the romantic quality of an ancient ruin. It had that particular vitality one finds at birth and death alike, and like that certain time of spring and fall which are almost indistinguishable. I knew if just *that* could be kept, it would be a fine house.

We somehow never got around to making detailed plans. The subject came up, of course, but what with the rush of getting things done (the house and landscape were complete and occupied one year after original decision) and the fun of improvising the detail, more than the original sketches and those developed on odd scraps of paper during construction seemed de trop. After an outline diagram, sufficient for filing with the building department, constant supervision replaced drawings.

The ordinary problems of construction were greatly alleviated by the owner-builder's know-how and his willingness to subordinate usual methods to the main theme which soon caught on and was reflected enthusiastically by the workmen and technicians. The big problem was in maintaining a rigid discipline against "tastes" and "inspirations" over so long a period without the benefit of written specifications. But under my own jealous eye, not too much went wrong—much less than I have seen on jobs that were all "paper," and little supervision.

Mistakes were made—in both workmanship and judgment. But who has built a house without them? I can see any number of things I would do differently if I had them to do over, but at least we avoided the terrifying prospect of having the house "decorated." When the clients began thinking of furnishings, I recommended an architect whose judgment I considered impeccable and for whose houses I had often designed landscapes. He not only assisted in furnishings, but designed all the cabinet work and assisted with technical problems as they arose. This represented a complete turnabout in the relations of architect and landscape architect—one which I enjoyed immensely.

I tried to make the basic concept responsive to nature—rather than the whims of people or the architectural preoccupation with a "house" as an entity. In this way, I thought it might continue a little longer to have the qualities of the beginning and the end.

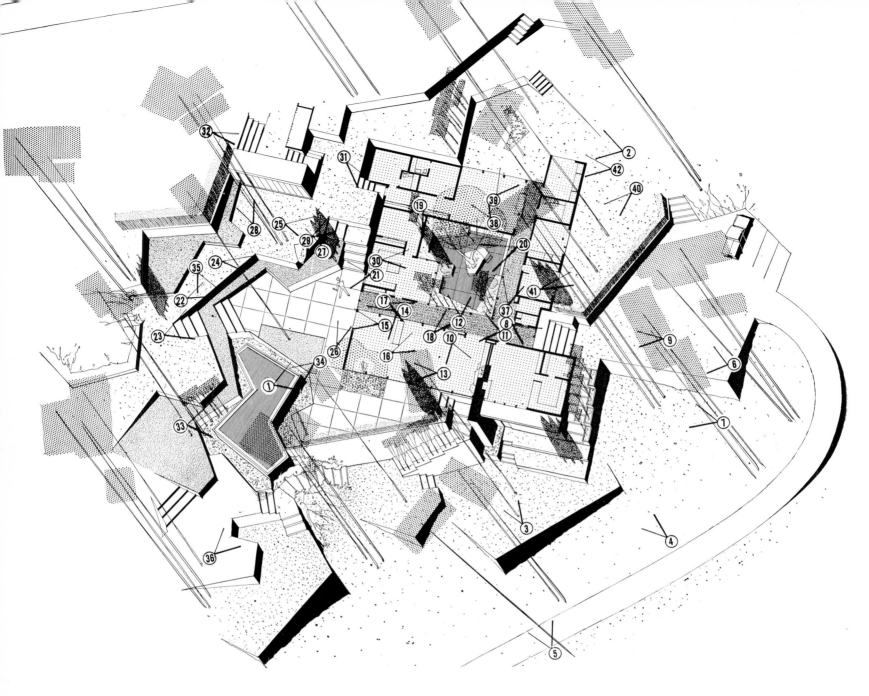

*Numbers refer
to photographs. 1956*

3

4

5

EXTERIORS

Views from entrance drive. Landscape is entirely remade, without disturbing natural growth, to accommodate large house comfortably. Terrace levels, retained by tie walls, give a horizontal feeling to steep slope, integrate the house with its natural surroundings, and give two-way privacy to activity beyond.

6

7

8

9

Side elevations (left, and above), as seen from motor court on arrival, maintains privacy of activity beyond: master bedroom is protected by solid vertical siding wall—children's bedrooms and adjoining gardens, by holly hedge above tie retaining wall.

Above, right, interior of entrance hall, looking outdoors, leads back to motor court and to outdoor stairway along bedroom façade (right) leading to lower levels and utilities.

LIVING ROOM

*From entrance hall, atrium appears on one's
right—conversational group around fireplace
(left) on left. Pool terraces are straight ahead.
Lowered egg crate ceiling
expresses communication with outdoors.*

Atrium—visually and spatially part of the living room—may be partially or completely shut off by sliding shoji to adjust the view or create plant silhouettes. When water is drained, area may be used as walled patio for entertaining.

13

Dining space is an integral part of the outdoors. Tile brasier under interior trellis (above), a convenience for informal serving indoors, communicates with living terrace, and pool. From dining table (below) one sees view to north (left of mural), and to garden-pool terraces (right of mural) as shown in picture opposite.

14

16

At left: view from interior trellis, looking back across living room toward entrance hall; atrium on left, fireplace group on right, and bridge table in foreground. Below: view from dining area, looking diagonally across living room toward entrance, fireplace group and terrace.

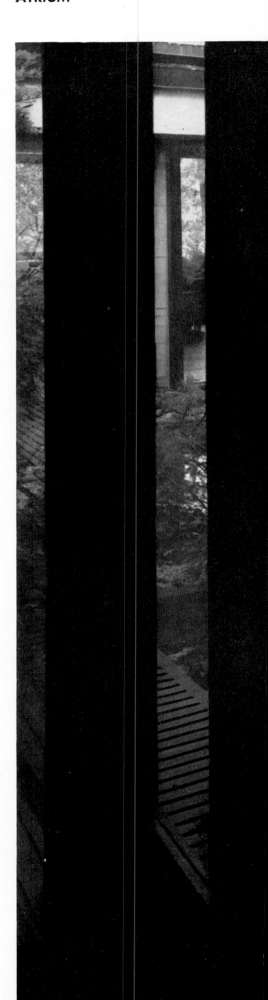

17

18

This bayou-like atrium, central to theme of both house and landscape, separates the three main divisions of layout—adult living, children's wing, and service—which surround it. View above, from living room, looks diagonally across to hallway off children's bedrooms; play room is directly behind blank white wall on far side. The down shot (below) taken from roof of service portion, looks back to the same hallway from opposite angle; living room is at right of picture concealed by evergreen cryptomeria trees. Kitchen door (extreme right of picture) opens on to atrium for service when water is drained and area is used as patio.

19

Looking back from hallway which connects children's bedrooms and playroom, one sees across atrium through living room, to landscape beyond. At extreme right is entrance to atrium from kitchen—kitchen activity is obscured by frosted glass.

20

21

TERRACES

Down-shot gives general view of terraces off dining area. Pool area is to the left of picture, bathhouses and service to the right. Stairway, leading to play field, enclosed by earth mound created to screen neighboring houses, begins a peripheral circuit system of the grounds connecting all levels and areas.

22

Bathhouses, left, and services, in background, surround snack terraces. Tie walls, at seat height, accommodate large gatherings. Central poised flat stone serves as buffet table accessible from different levels. Lanterns above.

Looking back toward dining-living space, the textured concrete pool terrace is central to the swimming pool, right, and bathhouses with cobblestone serving terrace, left. Spray jet decorates the terrace, cools the atmosphere as well as bathers. Terrace levels are carved and shaped to fit the levels of existing trees. Ground surfaces of wood chips, lower left, cobblestone and ground cover, blacktop, pebbles, and textured concrete—divided in 8' squares—foil the separation of levels, create rich textural effect. Lowered roof, center distance, expresses interior passageway between service, left, and master living, right.

23

24

Poised rock-buffet and terraces (above) in relation to interior passageway which divides interior dining space, right, from kitchen, left. Dining space window (opposite) reflects garden terraces approached by stairway. Trellis is an extension of interior trellis embracing hood over brasier. Evergreen holly hedge, on top of wall, divides service from garden spaces. Return to lower level (below) is accented by vertical and horizontal rocks used sculpturally. Upper and lower window strips admit light to kitchen while baffling servants' view to living terraces.

25

26

Natural rock, sculptural in quality, announces the entrance to bathhouse terrace, and acts as a foil against foliage as well as translucent and opaque construction.

Wall seat and flat rocks (below) indicate a conversational group adjacent to built-in bar behind vertical siding. Batten strips, continuous across siding and sunray glass, maintain architectural unity while admitting light. Access to bathhouses and bar is through doors in siding. Service parking and access from the alley above is obscured by planting and the structure itself.

27

28

Servants' dining space in kitchen, occasionally used by family for breakfast, is obscured from rest of house by frosted glass, but clear glass and door open to atrium for service and view. Passage between cabinet walls leads to laundry, servants' rooms, and service access from alley.

30

SERVICE

*From off-alley parking, the service enters via stairway
between back of bathhouses and storage wall (right).
Translucent panels obscure inner service court
from alley down-view. Left turn at baffle takes service
across court under lower trellis to steps at kitchen
and laundry entrance (above).*

View from one pool terrace back toward house and living terrace.
Split rock (below) forms multiple seat for bathers.

POOL

Shaped to fit between existing trees and to follow the slope of the land, the pool bottom steps down with the grade—the shallow portion, for children, in foreground. A plant moat surrounding water diminishes accident hazard, and serves as warning against unattended entry by children. Moat is crossed at specific points via tie bridges. Moat plants, water, and surrounding trees are illuminated at night. Dispersed terraces at tree root levels encourage large gatherings to distribute in smaller groups throughout the area. Pool edge is less than 100' from highway below.

*Peripheral circuit of slopes and terraces continues
around pool as fusion of house and landscape becomes apparent. Pool, held rigid by tie and earth dam,
projects into the wooded landscape where wood
chips are used for groundcover. Holly hedge, on top
of terrace retaining wall acts as balustrade, screens
activity from highway below; house curtains
are unnecessary winter or summer.*

CHILDREN

Children's area, as seen from entrance hall, may be closed off from the rest of the house by folding doors. At such times, the specific area of the entrance hall includes powder room (door on right). Beyond folding doors, the low ceiling divides children's bedrooms from atrium. Passage connects with play room (opposite) and outdoor play space (below).

39

Outdoor play space, divided into three levels, communicates with bedroom off children's gardens. Various levels are connected by ramps with woodland, back alley, and service area for storage of toys.

2

40

Private bedroom garden for two girls has access from their bedrooms. It is screened from the motor court (left, out of picture) by holly hedge with enclosure suggested by three Photinia trees and mountain laurel divider. Blacktop paving makes pattern in pebbles while dividing area in two more-or-less equal parts. Hieroglyphics by the children.

41

42

View from one of the children's bedrooms (upper right)
into their garden. Path leads to play yard off play room.
Detail (lower right) shows handling of pebbles and black-
top at corner of children's wing leading to play yard.

PART II

Definitions of Space

Immediately after World War II, I hired an assistant—largely on the basis of his having been stationed in Japan, and as army sergeant, placed in charge of "gardens." During our brief association, I could discover nothing in particular that had rubbed off on to the sergeant's garden consciousness from his experience. But after questioning, I was interested to learn that he had been in charge not of GIs, but of Japanese prisoners assigned to maintaining the Imperial Gardens in Tokyo.

My envy was hardly concealed—until he told of an old man in his crew who had been in charge of the Imperial Gardens during peace time. According to the sergeant's description, the old man had a long, but thin white beard, and a body bent almost double with age. But every time those "gooks" (as he called them) passed the old man, they bowed low, and removed their caps. "They never paid any attention to me," he said, "and I was a *sergeant*."

It is just such intimations that make me wonder about the American attitude toward gardens, and what, if anything, gardens could become to express our real character. I would like to be permitted a few assumptions. By assumptions, I mean pure guesses which I could not hope to prove in any scientific manner, but which, when lumped together, represent a belief or a theory from which to operate. My only justification has already been stated by Gideon in discussing the limitations of an historian's interpretation of a period: "No man of a later time . . . . can approach the direct and certain feeling for a period which belonged to those in the midst of the struggle—a struggle which involved their destiny. Words uttered out of the

needs of the time are the historian's real guides . . . . The true critique of an age can only be taken from the testimony of that age."

I am willing to hazard the guess that if you asked any roomful of people to give immediate associations with the word "garden," the predominant association would be "flowers." Other candidates, on the more or less joyful side, would be "springtime," "horticulture," "vegetables"; on the pessimistic side, "weeding," "backache," "insects." Less likely, but still possible, would be "enclosure," "privacy," and "relaxation." It would be an avant garde roomful, indeed, that came up with "sculpture," "space," or "space-sculpture."

On the other hand, assuming even a cursory knowledge of history, if you asked such a group to associate with "Renaissance Gardens," the word "flower" would probably not enter into it at all. More likely, it would run like, "bosco," "courtyard," "allée," "grotto," "fountain," "picture," and for those more technically familiar, "axis," and "perspective."

If you applied the same test to the words "Japanese Gardens," the associations would undoubtedly be more like, "tea ceremony," "symbolism," "nature-in-miniature," "Buddha," "rock composition," and for the more learned, "in yo," "gojo," "gog yo"—which have to do, mainly, with the principles and philosophy of garden making.

It would be impossible to make an intelligent guess as to what associations with "gardens" would predominate if such a test were given to a Renaissance or a Japanese group *at the time their gardens were being evolved*. It seems quite unlikely that the word would be "flowers," because flowers did not come to dominate the garden scene until much later—mostly in England.

I think the fact that, when we look at gardens from a little distance, we see their other and more enduring (or residual) characteristics is a good indication that these characteristics are more important than they appear to the amateur. It seems, also, that while it may be appropriate for the amateur to associate "garden" with "flowers," the connoisseur and the professional must begin their thinking with those elements which constitute its essence.

For instance, it is easy for us to see how the gardens of the Rennaissance were dominated and encompassed by the then new and fascinating discovery of perspective—from which developed a whole system of design admirably suited to the conditions of that day. Gardens were viewed from specific points where pictures were "composed" of landscape materials. Within this purely visual concept, the axial vista, connecting one formal area with the next, bordered on either side by the grand allée, fitted neatly into the pattern of a Medicean society or the court of Louis XIV. But most important, it gave elbow room to the creative horizon of the day.

If the Renaissance garden evolved from the discovery and exploitation of perspective, the Japanese garden certainly evolved from the need of the spirit. Untouched by the scientific discoveries of the Western Renaissance, the Japanese garden is the product of an insular culture and a medieval society working out its concept of deity in nature and natural forms. It is filled with the "secrets" of great gardeners, poets, and philosophers who revealed the mysteries of the universe in parables, symbols, and preachments which became the guiding rules of garden making.

But it must be remembered that the "rules" were the rules of poetry, and the rules of philosophy which found their truths in nature, and were popularly believed as well as practiced. Within such a working system it was possible to express the cardinal virtues of humanity,

justice, politeness, wisdom, and fidelity in garden forms. One could suggest the Buddhist deities by the grouping of rocks, and inspire the arrangement with content. The relative positions of heaven, earth, and man could become clear through symbols.

I think it would be difficult to find an approach to gardening more remote from the "main currents of American thought." And yet, the tranquillity, and the beauty, and the devotion of Japanese gardens have inspired the wonder of the world—including America. But Americans find this "spirit" deal a little hard to take, and rather than go through the tedium of the whole experience, would prefer going right to the horse's mouth—in this instance, Japan—and bring the gardens back to, say, Minnesota.

The popular notion that a culture can be transplanted casually by an arrangement of rocks, or the importation of Japanese gardeners, is caused not so much by lack of feeling as by a naïve belief in *"things"*—an attitude that should have dissipated itself with the importation of the first castle from Europe. But the belief is as strong, and sometimes as implacable, as the heart-rending certainty of my German Shepherd that I am somehow locked in the telephone, because he hears my voice over it, when I am away from home. However touching mistaken beliefs may be, I think we must reach for a more valid relation between our own cultural roots and their outward expression before we can lay claim to gardens that at once do us credit and are truly indigenous. Our national attitude toward gardens, essentially agricultural, in itself seems healthy enough—at least "earthy." The well-kept farm, orchard, and vineyard, like the fine old barns that often accompany gingerbread farm houses, are usually superior to the self-conscious attempts to do something "artistic." In its lowest form this impulse leads to the whitewashed stones along the drive and automobile tires filled with petunias on the front lawn. But occasionally anonymous little gardens can be found that have the indigenous quality of folk art and, like folk music, have an organic quality and feeling that cannot be denied or ignored; here are the threads from which the fabric of a fine art may some day be woven.

The purely agricultural approach, however, overlooks the fact that we are no longer an agricultural nation, and the purpose of gardens is no longer just to grow plants and flowers, but to create the kind of space that will orient the individual to nature in a mechanized civilization. What kind of space will do this? Certainly not the legislated kind which we already have and which does not relieve the barrenness of our communities—urban or rural. I believe it will have to be a concept—a framework of thinking, if you will—that gives direction to the design of contemporary gardens as the discovery of perspective gave impetus to the gardens of the Renaissance, and the deification of nature gave a unique quality to the gardens of Japan.

I do not believe for a moment that any manipulation of the physical environment can be fully effective until it fuses with the social and economic patterns of society—as well as the patterns of nature—but I see nothing wrong with beginning in one's own back yard. And in considering the space in one's own back yard, the emphasis, both legal and individual, is at present on one dimension only—the ground surface —whereas, in capturing the sense of space, we are always dealing with the volume—surface, sides, and top.

These elements are more difficult to handle effectively out of doors than they are under the roof of a house because of the relatively great horizontal dimensions, the infinite expanse of the sky, and the tendency to ignore what cannot be touched. But it is quite necessary to use some kind of yardstick by which this dimension and this infinity can be measured and consciously felt to produce a garden.

I have often thought that most of the garden design problems would be solved if we started with a sky plan rather than a ground plan. The sky is really the ceiling of a garden, and more

accurately so called, in its original sense, than is the top of a room because our word *ceiling* comes from the Latin *caelum* meaning heaven or sky. But, while in a room some kind of top is more or less forced on us by construction, outdoors the sense of sky must be made real by consciously arranging the overhead pattern so that we become aware of the sky as a ceiling. This can be done by as simple a device as the branches of trees overhead. But man-made constructions—trellises for growing vines, sculptural canopies, and solid shelter for protection from the elements—serve the same end if, aside from their utilitarian purpose, the intention is to bring the sky into the garden.

If you have a sky pattern, however it is achieved, you have already the beginning of the sides of this volume: you have the tree trunks coming from the ground, you have the walls or vertical supports for trellises, canopies, or shelter, you have begun to define space, you have a sense of enclosure. This need not be a continuous and arbitrary band or fence around the property, but simple divisions which may be loose or dense, solid or perforated, transparent, translucent, or opaque. But they must always be considered in relation to the eye level; you can look at them, over them, or through them. The ultimate reason for having these divisions is as much for psychic comfort as for practical solution to a problem, but the trick is to turn the problem into a comfort, and I have tried to illustrate this throughout the book.

The most important point, and the one most likely to be overlooked, is that the openings in the "sides" are as important as the sides themselves and should also have a reason. The reason may be as simple and practical as gaining a means of access to the space. Or it could be to admit light, to open a view, or to create the feeling of continuing space. Whatever the reason, there is an interplay between these voids (openings) and solids (materials). In the total volume, the space is being carved by the materials, and, as in sculpture, the value of the result depends largely on the (interspatial) balance that is achieved in terms of the "problem" involved.

To complete this volume of space, a surface (or floor) is needed. I have purposely said little about surfaces until now in an attempt to counteract what I consider to be a distorted emphasis on them. Everyone loves surfaces—the way everyone loves flowers—but they do not make a garden. In its proper context, the surface is the earth—a fluid and plastic material that, in a garden, has to be adapted to two basic purposes: the needs of people, and the needs of plants—the rest is sculpture.

From the point of view of people, the most overlooked factor is that the surface must be level for most uses; it is impossible, or at least uncomfortable to eat at a table, sit on a chair, or throw a ball on a surface that is not substantially level. The most permanent and durable surfaces (to say nothing of the most popular) are the standard "hard" materials, like brick or flagstone, laid in cement. And herein lies a conflict because most plants grow best in a loose spongy strata that holds moisture. My own solution to this impasse is usually a combination of "hard" and "soft" materials laid "dry" (imbedded in sand rather than concrete) which permits the paving to act as a mulch for plants while providing a hard surface to walk on. And here, again, the trick is to express this conflict in patterns that unify the two opposing functions.

I usually tend to think of this volume concept of space-sculpture as something that, with luck, may be applied to a barren suburban lot that has been plundered by a developer, and then legally sterilized. I have been conditioned to thinking that way: it is the usual scene. But space-sculpture might be better understood if thought of as a civilized method of invading the unspoiled terrain.

Let us assume such an unspoiled terrain, heavily wooded, with naturally undulating ground. It would be a simple matter, using the tools or machinery at our disposal, to hack away at plants and ground forms until, as Michelangelo said of marble, the image of sculpture appeared. In this instance, it would be the balance of elements in space surrounding man in all directions with nature adapted to his needs in such a way that he became more aware of it. Portions of the undulating ground would, of necessity, be leveled for comfort and for use, and the sides (trees and growth) would be modified for circulation and enjoyment. The woodland scene, so to speak, would bear the same relation to its original condition as a flower arrangement bears to a field of wildflowers.

I can sense the immediate reaction that wildflowers in a field are to be preferred to any "arrangement," and I must admit their charm and interest, but at the same time I cannot escape a revulsion toward this attitude. It is the same sticky sentiment that makes us see gardens, and the landscape generally, as something you "add on" or exclude entirely from the serious and "grown up" business of building a house or a city. And it is difficult to see why we are so sentimental about, or oblivious of, *arranging* nature in our living environment when we think nothing of destroying it entirely.

But since we are dealing in assumptions, let us assume that we do arrange this unspoiled terrain so that it has the qualities of psychic comfort and so that it does capture space in a way that could be called sculptural. All that is lacking is shelter—the protective top or ceiling, and an "arrangement" of side walls for enclosure—to have a house.

I say "house" because we do not have an individual word in the American language to describe the fusion of shelter with the landscape, but if the need for it should ever become recognized, we would probably get the word. And who knows? With such a word, we might build a whole community of space-sculpture-with-shelter, instead of houses-plus-gardens. It might even spread to cities, this fusion idea, and then we would have a lot of people going from one place to another and carrying on their business and living right in the midst of nature instead of preserving that dream patch of wildflowers somewhere else. It would be like going sane.

Ceilings

A trellis is a man-made tree. It may have vines or not, but as a tree, its function in the humanized landscape is to make us aware of the sky, to bring the sky into the garden.

Wild cherry tree creating its own patterns against night sky.

Trellis and tree canopy— symbols of man in nature.

Cultivated grape vine creates sky pattern with trellis and trees.

This "man-made tree," entirely of steel, is designed to withstand the attack of wisteria.

BY TWINING STEMS	Flower	Fruit	Sun or shade	Remarks
Bower Actinidia *Actinidia arguta*	July—small white, fragrant	Sept. yellow green edible	either	vigorous dioecious
Oriental Bittersweet *Celastrus orbiculata*		Oct. orange	either	dioecious vigorous to destructive
Chinese Fleece Vine *Polygonum auberti*	Sept.–Oct. white		full sun	prune back each spring
Kudzu bean	July–August purple		full sun	fast, vigorous, no pests, withstands drought, perennial in cold climates
Chinese Wisteria *Wisteria sinensis*	May—lavender, white, pink, before foliage racemes 1′	pods	sun	dioecious vigorous to destructive
Japanese Wisteria *Wisteria floribunda*	June–July, after foliage racemes 3′	pods	sun	dioecious vigorous to destructive
BY CLINGING AERIAL ROOTLETS	Flower	Fruit	Sun or shade	Remarks
Trumpet creeper *Campsis radicans*	July Aug.–Sept. orange	pods	full sun	attracts hummingbirds
English Ivy *Hedera helix baltica*	Evergreen		shade	gracilis is best cut leaf variety
Boston Ivy		Aug.–Nov. black fruit red leaves	either	
Virginia Creeper		Sept.–Oct. blue fruit red leaves	sun or light shade	
BY COILING TENDRILS	Flower	Fruit	Sun or shade	Remarks
Porcelain Ampelopsis *Ampelopsis brevipedunculata*		Sept.–Oct. porcelain blue	sun light shade	
Clematis	July–Aug. various		full sun	henryi recommended white
Grape		Sept.–Oct. purple, blue, green	full sun	

VINES

The purpose of a trellis is to make a sky pattern, support a vine, and cast a shadow. Almost any vine will grow on almost any trellis. The vine can be tied up or tied down to make it hang right. You can make a bush like forsythia or a tree like dogwood grow like a vine with proper training. And this is an interesting thing to do. But ordinary vines, themselves, grow in different ways and should have trellises adapted to their method of growth.

By twining stems, these, like wisteria and bittersweet, will twine their stems around anything or around other stems and are often destructive. An open, free standing construction is best for support so that the vine will show off to advantage and will not tear away parts of the house.

By aerial rootlets, like the ivies and the trumpet creeper, these have small roots above ground which attach themselves to a flat, slightly rough surface such as a brick wall.

By coiling tendrils, like grapes and clematis, they must have something less than half inch in diameter to hold on to: rope, wire or thin slats of wood.

By suction, certain vines, such as euonymus, will climb two stories of a flat surface with no visible means of holding on. They have neither twining stems, rootlets, or tendrils, but if you pull them away from the surface, they will snap back by suction.

Delicate tendrils of clematis coil around thin nylon parachute cord.

Common grape, more vigorous, and requiring constant pruning, can be trained to a more open trellis.

Sides

Opposite: bamboo roll screen (outside peel) fastened to vertical mullions with lath strips. Will last in northern climate better than five years if painted with clear oil paint to preserve cord between slats. Planting is flowering dogwood, willow, and hanging basket of petunias. Street and sidewalk are three feet beyond.

Above: translucent plastic shoji panels, set in frames, are removable.

Below: combination of plastic and bamboo in pattern divisions of frames in two foot modules.

STRUCTURAL SIDES

Plants and construction combine in the division of space. Above: alternate plank fence admits light and air while obscuring the view beyond. Espalier pear trees give decorative form. Left: twisted bamboo and form of linden tree are open enough to permit interspatial vista, enriching the view beyond.

Right: detail of alternate plank fence construction.
Below: twisted bamboo, in series, gives sense of enclosure decoratively,
plays with sunlight, filters artificial illumination at night.

PLANTING AS SPACE DIVIDERS

The strawberry guava trees (left) in California, and the white birch throughout the northeast are outstanding examples of the tracery form in trees. They divide space while not obscuring vision. Recalling the same forms in the distance gives a sense of enclosure and direction. Note the intimate relation between plant "sides" and surface textures.

SCULPTURAL SIDES

Above and right are two halves of the same rock poised in the landscape as sculptural seats.

Picture opposite shows sculptural ground modeling to differentiate between levels. The tracery of honey locusts combine with a casual planting of day lilies and a surface of large pebbles to complete the division.

Basket-weave brick and square-cut flagstone platforms recall rectangular shape of pool. Levels separate bathers from nonbathers.

STEPS

Steps are a transition between sides and surfaces in the definition of space. When the tread is broadened, it becomes a useable surface; and risers, in series, become a side wall. By combining these two factors, steps—or changes in level —become integral with the total garden space.

Random-spaced steps make transition between natural surroundings and stereotyped pool. . . . . create terrace levels and spaces for living.

Enlarged tread, surfaced in flagstone, provides raised dais for outdoor dining.

Levels carved in natural landscape make nature useable.

Textured concrete, marked off in 22-inch squares by a combination of redwood two-by-fours and line grouting, gives a subtle sense of direction, and step forms make easy transition to lawn area.

"Informal" steps are made of thin, precast concrete slabs balanced on concrete triangular strips (see diagram). Height of riser can be adjusted from four to six inches by turning triangular strips onto the proper base during construction.

*Raised beds, steps, and plant walls of ties
in a field of tan pebbles, grey slate squares,
and groundcover give form to the natural
landscape.*

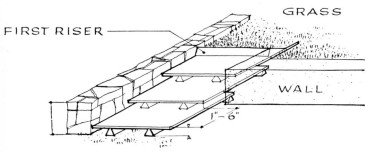

FIRST RISER

GRASS

WALL

1"–6"

Surfaces

Patio block—
2 × 8 × 16"
laid dry.

Textured concrete—
with open joints
for drainage

Water—*dark like a bayou*

Blacktop—*pervious to water—*
can be brought to tree trunk.

Textured concrete—*with 2 × 4" redwood strips.*

Mixed pebbles—
sun pattern.

Water—*placid*

Water—*reflecting*

Water—*activated*

Grass carpet in bluestone squares.

Wood chips in the woodland.

Surfaces in succession:
plants, water,
blacktop, wood chips, pebbles.

Grey slate, tan pebbles, and creosoted wood plant box.

Slate has a mosaic of its own.

Rough texture—one and one-half inch crushed bluestone.

Bluestone chips—
streaked with birch shadows.

In this winter scene, one has the sense of the earth. The grass and flagstone forms have a positive and negative relationship vignetted into the trees and the rise in ground. . . . .

opposite, the same principles are used in a more geometric pattern.

Tie cross sections, sand, and ivy. Certain ties are raised slightly to provide steps and take up the slope in the ground.

The floor is the earth. In a garden, it accommodates plants and the activity of people. It also has a character of its own—responsible to the natural law; it may be modified, but not changed, and before modifying its surface too extensively, it might be well to consider some of the advantages and disadvantages. Usually, the cost is a mighty conditioner since it will often be fifty times more per square foot for, say, flagstone in concrete than for loose pebbles. And one is not better than the other—except in context. The only maxim is that surfaces should never be considered alone; they should relate to the space divisions and the sky.

HARD ROCK—flagstone, brick, cobble, tile, stone, patio block, wood disks, precast concrete.

Laid dry, in sand

Advantages
Acts as plant mulch; easily rearranged in pattern; less expensive than concrete.

Disadvantages
More difficult to lay properly; inclined to heave with frost if improperly laid.

Laid in concrete

Advantages
More precision possible; permanent and durable.

Disadvantages
Withholds moisture from plants; irrevocable in pattern; more expensive.

FLUID TYPES—mixed and poured, or spread, into place before solidifying —like asphalt and concrete.

Pervious to water (untreated asphalt)

Advantages
Acts as plant mulch; resilient surface; inexpensive; easily fitted to ground modulations.

Disadvantages
Relatively soft; will show furniture marks; some weed control necessary.

Impervious to water (concrete and sealed asphalt types)

Advantages
Permanent hard surface; can be moulded accurately.

Disadvantages
Needs special provisions for plant watering; inflexible after set.

LOOSE MATERIAL—spread on like a mulch.

Hard particles—pebbles, crushed stone, decomposed granite, sand, pulverized brick, marble chips.

Advantages
Inexpensive; excellent plant mulch; adaptable in form; tactual resilience; colorful, clean appearance.

Disadvantages
Requires some weed control; must be kept raked to look well; will disperse, requires stiff edging to keep in place.

Soft particles—organic material, such as wood chips, pine needles, sawdust, buckwheat hulls, tanbark, pine cones.

Advantages
Excellent mulch; inexpensive; natural appearance.

Disadvantages
Soggy when wet; may cling; requires renewal.

GROWING VEGETATION
—that may be walked on—grass mixtures and dicondra

Advantages
Fine appearance; uniform texture; lively color when properly cared for; prevents erosion.

Disadvantages
Installation expensive; maintenance eternal; looks well only at a distance, or when perfectly kept.

—that may not be walked on—groundcovers, mosses, ferns.
Advantages
Prevents erosion; generally good appearance; can be combined with flowers and bulbs for seasonal interest.

Disadvantages
None.

WATER—placid and activated—purely of the spirit.

Iris . . . a structural flower.

GROUNDCOVERS AND FLOWERS

Flowers and groundcovers combine with man-made surfaces to make the garden floor. I would like to suggest a half dozen flowers that have interesting form, require little care, look well when not in bloom, blossom every year and continue the flower interest throughout the growing season: narcissi, lilies of the valley, irises, day lilies, oriental poppies, chrysanthemums.

There are innumerable varieties within each group. In addition to wildflowers, annuals, and blossoming woody plants, this is an adequate list for anyone who "likes flowers," but not with full-time devotion.

EVERGREEN GROUNDCOVERS	Sun or shade	Bloom	Fruit & foliage
Wintercreeper *Euonymus fortunei* *radicans*	either		
Wintergreen *Gaultheria procumbens*	light shade	July–Aug. pink-white	Oct.–Nov. red berries red foliage
English Ivy *Hedera helix baltica*	full sun light shade		
Mazus japonicus	sun light shade	May red flower spikes	Oct. bronze coloring
Partridgeberry *Mitchella repens*	light shade	June pink-white	Aug.–Sept. red fruit
Pachistima canbyi	either		
Japanese Pachysandra *Pachysandra terminalis*	shade		
Thyme *Thymus sp.*	full sun	June–July lilac clusters	
Periwinkle *Vinca minor*	either	May–June blue	

Grass, brick, groundcover, perennials, and vine—interwoven . . . opposite: fabric of surfaces and sides.

Plant Forms

The only possible explanation for suburban planting is the nursery catalog. I have given a great deal of thought to the subject, and no matter what angle I approach it from, or how charitable I try to be, I always arrive at the same conclusion: the nursery catalog.

One day the housewife takes a critical look at her grounds. The lawn looks like the very devil, of course, but so does the neighbor's, and she's given up on that, anyway. The foundation planting at least hides the foundation. Now if there were only something to hide the foundation planting. . . .

But let's face it. It is a dull little piece of suburbia—not at all like anything they show in the magazines. It needs something. Color, perhaps, or more planting.

The steps that follow are something like the frustrations of Alice Adams trying to enliven her brown little living room with a dozen roses. Out comes the nursery catalog—well calculated to appease the frustration with a thousand colored blooms larger than life and infinitely more permanent—an exotic wonderland of perpetual color and enchantment.

Under the circumstances, and with the prices so right, an order is inevitable. But, confronted with so much enchantment, it is difficult to know where to stop. That has also been thought of in the catalog. For it offers a complete package, one of each, with hardly a single joy omitted. In the housewife's mind the place looks better already.

Then one day, quite unexpectedly, an enormous package arrives, burlap bound, containing dried branches of heaven knows what. There are also smaller packages of dried roots and excelsior and additional odd items all looking equally dead. Obviously something has to be done.

So, the next week end the whole family turns to, under the direction of the housewife, who by now is in a very poor position to admit that she does not know what is going on. With ordinary luck and no water, everything will die. But, un-

happily, we are saddled with the survival instinct, and suburban planting is born.

Is there a need to describe suburban planting? It is not an unfamiliar thing like space or gardens. The commuter sees it every day, and toils with it on week ends. There is the pink dogwood, and forsythia, of course (gives you such a lift in the spring); and a star magnolia (they say it will be a tree some day); and a crabapple (very choice, the catalogue says); and those two evergreens (I think one is a spruce or a hemlock); and a shade tree, probably a maple (not doing so well, it never had leaves); and a bunch of evergreen azaleas (yes, purple); and a mock orange; and a spirea; and a Weigela; and a rose of Sharon. (These are shrubs. Continuous bloom, you know). Oh, yes. A lilac. (I love lilacs). Watch out for that one! A red maple (very expensive). Well, now that you have seen the front yard, would you like to see the rear?

I do not want to give the impression that all suburban plantings are exactly alike. They vary enormously. It is amazing the variety you can get by planting one plant of each kind. They vary in cost, too; some use holly instead of Weigela. But the method is the same, and it is therefore, basically, the same kettle of fish.

Now, in all the history of horticulture, nothing worthwhile, from a design point of view, has been accomplished by this method; its premise is that the possession of materials is enough in itself, and more important than what you do with them. But it must be admitted that there are many points of view about plants: the botanist sees them under a microscope; the tree surgeon for their symmetry; the nurseryman as something to sell; the builder as something to clear from the site; the ecologist in relation to their environment; and the housewife thinks of them as flowers. I, personally, have a firm conviction that everyone who deals with plants is slightly insane, and my own mania toward them is that I think of them as something to *use*—as the painter uses paint and a

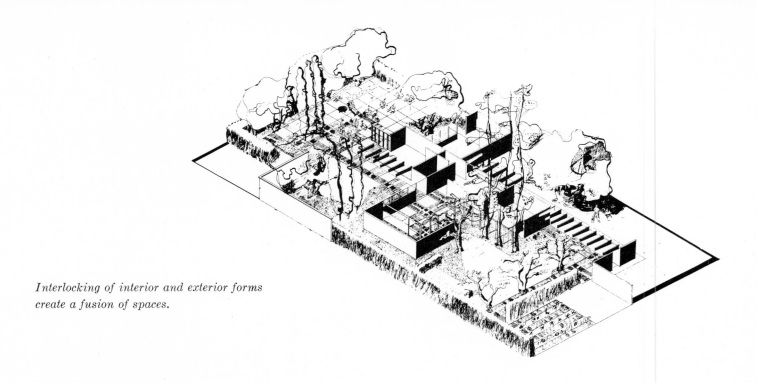

*Interlocking of interior and exterior forms
create a fusion of spaces.*

sculptor uses stone—to create the image of the world as the world should be: specifically, to create space in the landscape.

From the point of view of using them architecturally, the great maze of plants must be classified for that purpose. This eliminates a vast quantity. For instance, many fine plants such as the common sassafras cannot be moved in effective sizes. Another simplification is my own prejudice against certain horticulturally developed types such as some arborvitae and retinosperas.

On the other hand, I manage always to confuse the workmen on a job, and sometimes the client, by having no prejudice whatever against the currently despised ailanthus—the tree that grows in Brooklyn and is commonly known as the stink weed. Along with the ancient Chinese, I find it a truly beautiful tree, and one of the few exotics that grow in northern climates. In fact, it grows so fast and abundantly that the nurseries cannot sell it, which might account for their prejudice. However, they refuse to propagate the weeping mountain ash, which certainly would sell, on the theory that it is easier to extinguish a plant than to get rid of the borer which attacks it. This is slightly inconsistent since they have also gotten rid of the best trees that grow in this region—including the yellowwood, the scholar tree, cryptomeria and styrax—which have no more troubles than dogwood, if as many. I have stubbornly kept

these plants on my list, however, because I do find a hidden specimen occasionally and I still have the ridiculous fantasy of finding a nurseryman who is steadfast enough to produce them. But I do not value simplification enough to take the average nurseryman's way out, and eliminate everything except what can be carried in the back of a station wagon or is the equivalent of a Norway maple.

The following classification is a frame of reference categorizing plants for organic use. In the charts I suggest a few plants in each group to illustrate the method of selection.

Height—First in importance is the classification as to height—their relation to the human body. They are above or below the eye level. It will be immediately argued that plants do not remain the same height. True enough. I have seen mountain laurel as big as dogwood, and American holly as large as oak. But exceptions have no place in a classification, and classifications are meant to be destroyed as soon as they are understood. Plants do have a normal size range during mature growth just as people do, but some plants can also be held within convenient bounds for landscape purposes. For instance, the hemlock, although an eighty foot tree in the woods, can easily be kept at eight feet indefinitely. So, for this classification, the heights are those at which the plant will remain for a period of from ten to twenty years either by itself or with assistance:

below the eye level	above the eye level	
1–3'	6–12'	20–40'
3–6'	12–20'	40' plus

Form—Most plants grow in a sufficiently definite shape so that the experienced eye can identify them from outline alone. It is, therefore, possible to reduce further the confusing mass of vegetation to form-types.

Columnar	Broad and Spreading
Horizontal	Irregular and Picturesque
Round or Oval	Pendulous or Weeping

I have arbitrarily eliminated from this classification such well defined form-types as the conical, the vase shape, and other candidates which either do not occur often enough to make a classification, or I do not use in a form sense.

It will be noted that several plants fall into more than one form category i.e., dogwood is by natural growth extremely horizontal in character, but it is readily available in irregular and picturesque forms, the grafted types are often pendulous, and nursery grown stock, due to archaic practices, are sometimes round like an apple on a stick. Other plants respond well to clipping or pruning so that, for instance, the European sycamore, normally a broad and spreading tree above 40 feet, can be clipped, as is the custom in Europe, to a flat head which would place it in the horizontal category at a height of either 12 to 20, or 20 to 40 feet depending on the height to which it is clipped.

Spacing—Useful classifications emerge from this form palette, but since they are really suggestions for arrangement, or grouping in series, they are kept separate:

Tracery	Fenestration
Clumps	Hedges
Canopy	Baffles

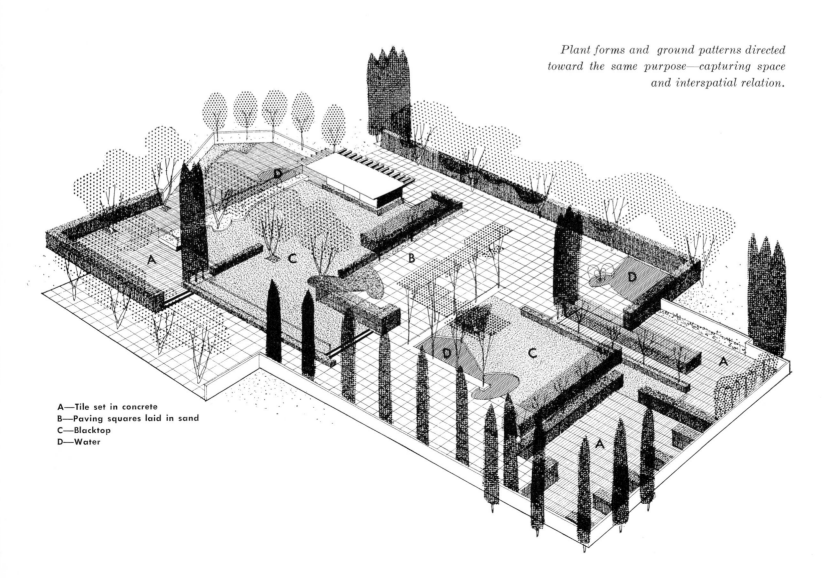

Plant forms and ground patterns directed toward the same purpose—capturing space and interspatial relation.

A—Tile set in concrete
B—Paving squares laid in sand
C—Blacktop
D—Water

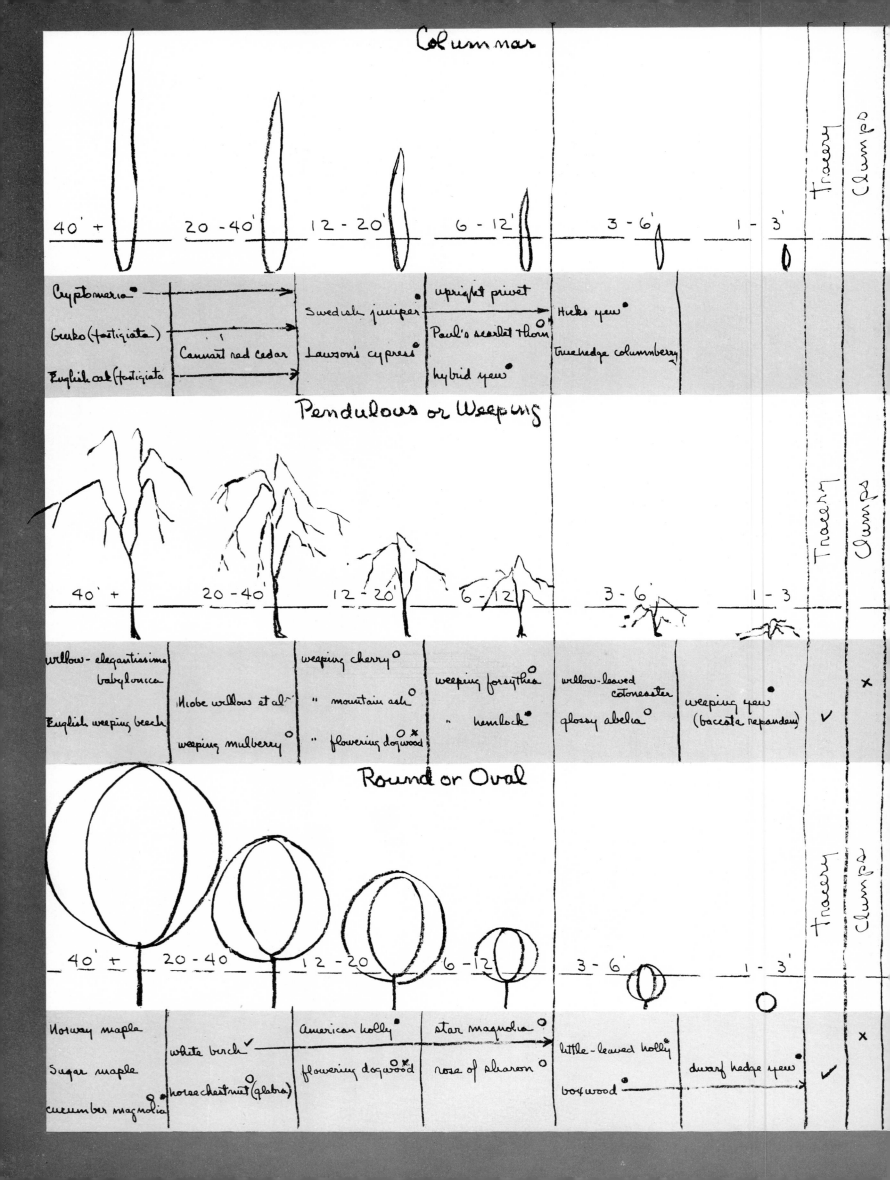

Columnar

40'+	20-40'	12-20'	6-12'	3-6'	1-3'	Tracery	Clumps
Cryptomeria●	→	Swedish juniper ●	upright privet	Hicks yew●			
Ginko (fastigiata)	Cannart red cedar	Lawson's cypress ●	Paul's scarlet thorn ○✗	Truehedge columnberry			
English oak (fastigiata)	→		hybrid yew●				

Pendulous or Weeping

40'+	20-40'	12-20'	6-12'	3-6'	1-3'	Tracery	Clumps
willow - elegantissima babylonica		weeping cherry ○	weeping forsythia ○	willow-leaved cotoneaster	weeping yew (baccata repandens) ●		✗
	Niobe willow et al	" mountain ash ○	" hemlock ●	glossy abelia ○		✓	
English weeping beech	weeping mulberry ○	" flowering dogwood ○✗					

Round or Oval

40'+	20-40'	12-20'	6-12'	3-6'	1-3'	Tracery	Clumps
Norway maple	white birch ✓	American holly ●	star magnolia ○	little-leaved holly ●	dwarf hedge yew ●		✗
Sugar maple	horse chestnut (glabra) ○	flowering dogwood ○✗	rose of sharon ○	boxwood ● →		✓	
cucumber magnolia ●							

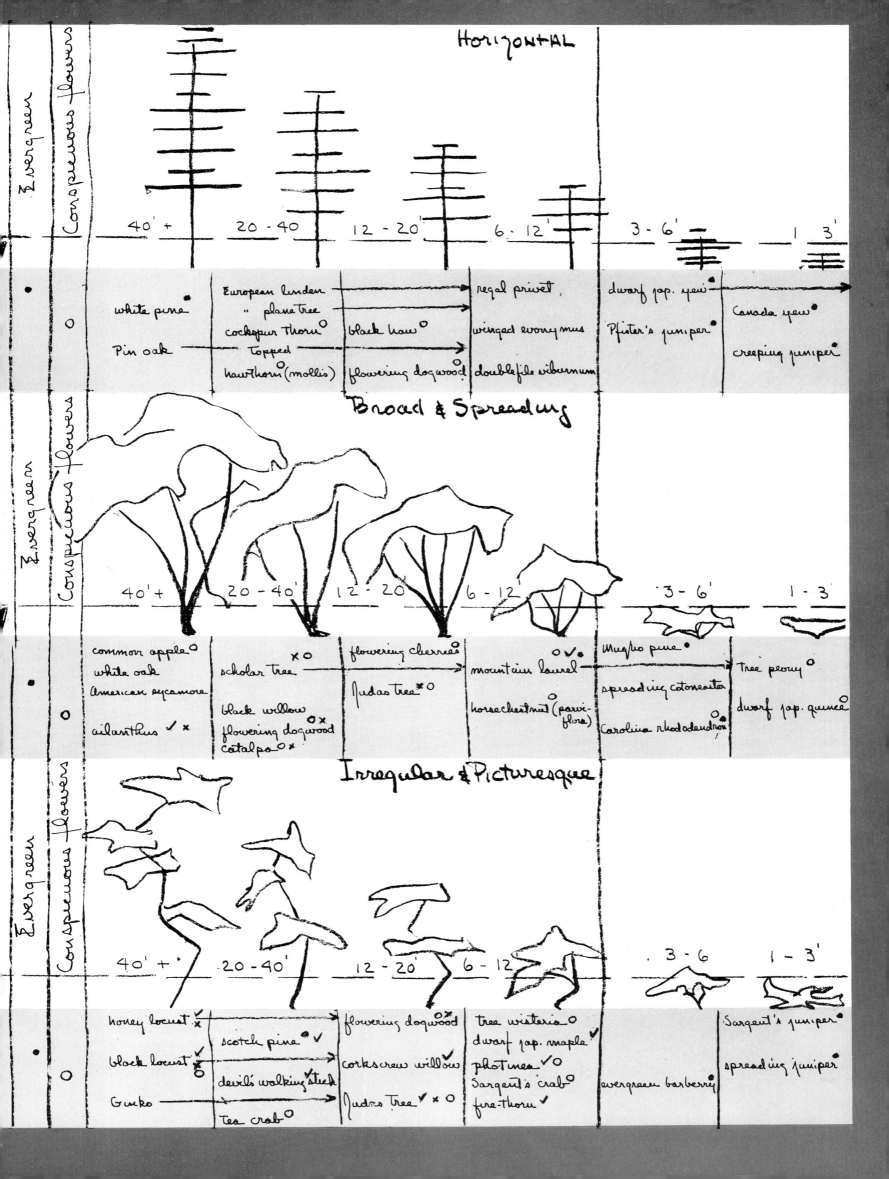

HORIZONTAL

Evergreen — Conspicuous flowers

40'+ | 20-40 | 12-20' | 6-12' | 3-6' | 1-3'

white pine — European linden, " plane tree, cockspur Thorn, Topped hawthorn (mollis) — regal privet, winged evonymus, doublefile viburnum — dwarf jap. yew, Pfister's juniper — Canada yew, creeping juniper
Pin oak — black haw, flowering dogwood

Broad & Spreading

Evergreen — Conspicuous flowers

40'+ | 20-40' | 12-20 | 6-12' | 3-6' | 1-3

common apple, white oak, American sycamore, ailanthus — scholar Tree, black willow, flowering dogwood, catalpa — flowering cherries, Judas tree — mountain laurel, horsechestnut (parvi-flora) — Mugho pine, spreading cotoneaster, Carolina rhododendron — Tree peony, dwarf jap. quince

Irregular & Picturesque

Evergreen — Conspicuous flowers

40'+ | 20-40' | 12-20 | 6-12' | 3-6 | 1-3'

honey locust, black locust, Ginko — scotch pine, devil's walking stick, Tea crab — flowering dogwood, corkscrew willow, Judas Tree — tree wisteria, dwarf jap. maple, photinea, Sargent's crab, fire-thorn — evergreen barberry — Sargent's juniper, spreading juniper

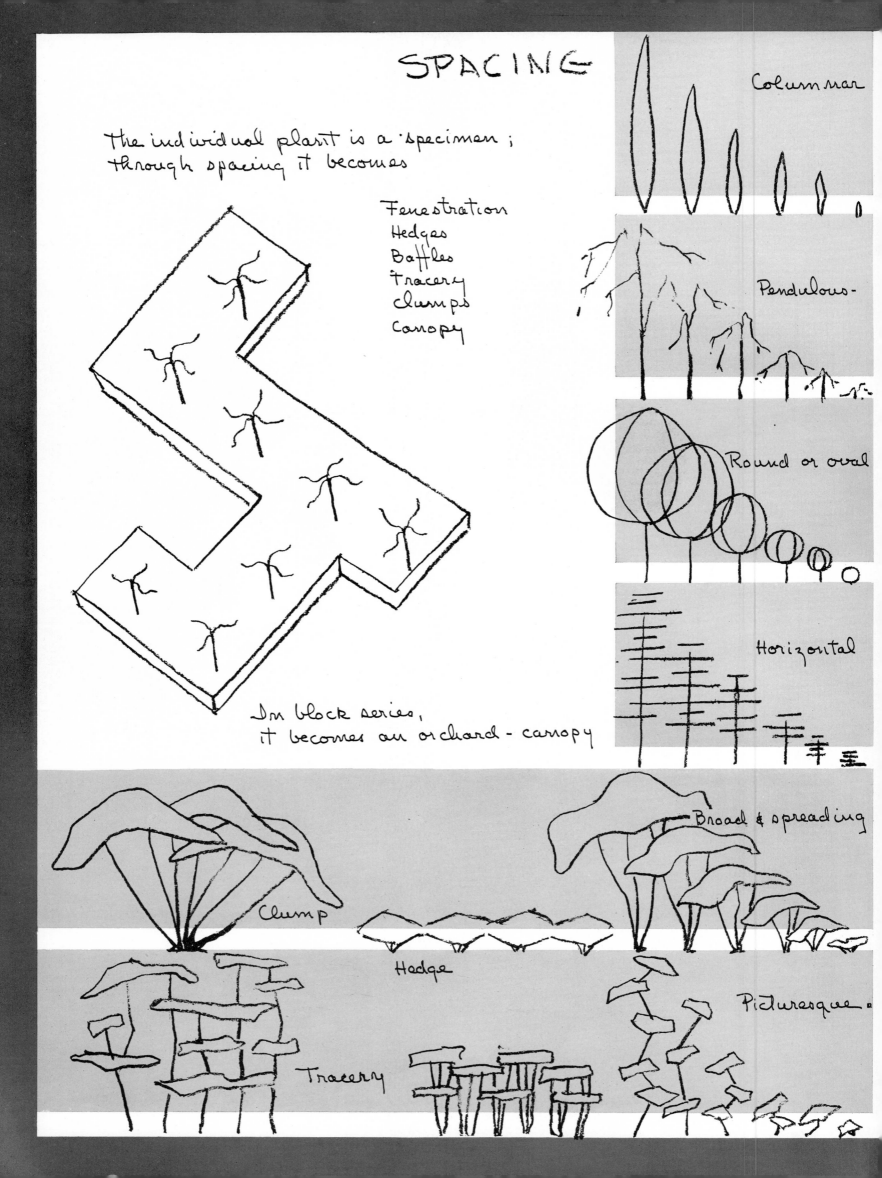

SPACING

The individual plant is a specimen; through spacing it becomes

Fenestration
Hedges
Baffles
Tracery
Clumps
Canopy

In block series, it becomes an orchard - canopy

Columnar

Pendulous-

Round or oval

Horizontal

Clump

Hedge

Broad & spreading

Tracery

Picturesque.

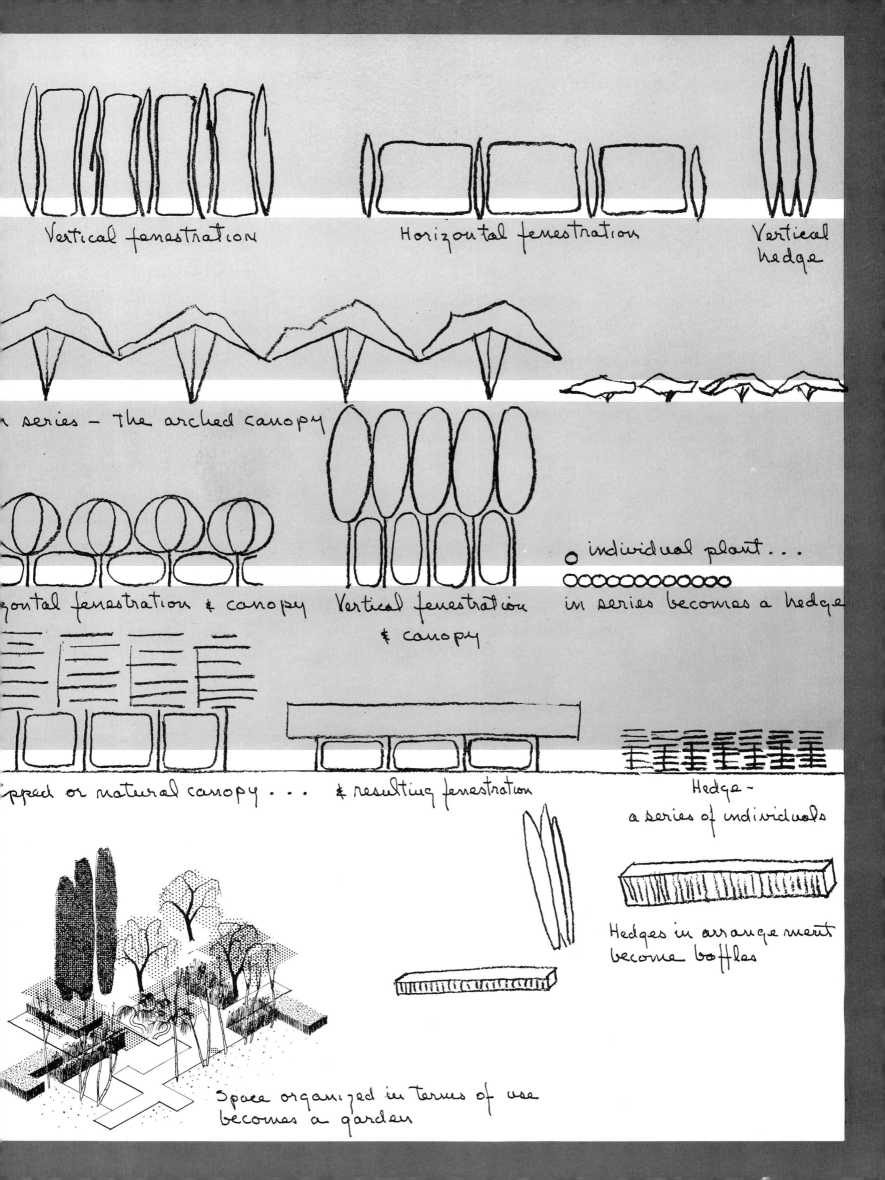

Vertical fenestration

Horizontal fenestration

Vertical hedge

n series — the arched canopy

zontal fenestration & canopy

Vertical fenestration & canopy

o individual plant...

in series becomes a hedge

pped or natural canopy... & resulting fenestration

Hedge — a series of individuals

Hedges in arrangement become baffles

Space organized in terms of use becomes a garden

How to Prevent a Garden

I have been warned, directly and indirectly, by innumerable publishers and editors that no book on the subject of gardens could possibly make its way unless it were a how-to-do-it—a manual that the homeowner could take with him into the back yard and start digging. I have no objection to the book being used in this way, although I would recommend a spade as a better vehicle, but it would seem to me that a few hours spent in contemplation before digging might be more profitable, and save at least the labor which no one wants to do, anyway.

I think it is possible to explain how to lay bricks or plant a shrub, and there are many good books which do just this, but to tell someone, whose place you have never seen, how to design a garden is like a doctor trying to perform an appendectomy over the telephone when he is not sure that the patient has appendicitis.

It occurred to me that a little preventative landscaping might be of more value, ultimately, and in this way I would not offend the how-to exponents and, at least to that degree, insure that the book would make its way.

I have, therefore, taken the trouble to classify the major ways in which a homeowner can prevent a garden from happening. I am not unaware that some of the individual items are well understood and much practiced, but the very broadness of a classification will bring at least a few items to the closer attention of garden lovers everywhere.

1 By Hard Labor

The left field technique. Get off into one corner of the property and build a barbecue or a rockery.
The studious application. Read all the books on growing flowers and plant all the flowers you read about. Make it depend on flowers. The test of success is when you find yourself saying, "If you had only come last month . . ."

2 By Attitudes

The plant lover's. Think of it as a menagerie of plants rather than a space for people. Get catalog fever in the spring and order an old fashioned potpourri.
The historic. Have fixed ideas about what a garden looks like and adapt the site to it. Visions of Spanish tile or roses climbing over a rustic fence will do equally well.
Cautious. Worship that "finished" look of respectability. What will the neighbors think? Plant a lawn with foundation planting.

3 Without Thinking At All

Ignore the sun and the sky, especially the shadows.
Have it open to the street and neighbors.
Ignore activity and circulation.
Clear and level the site.
Listen to everyone who knows a thousand ways it cannot be done.
Get all the accessories and decorations, especially lots of furniture, and forget about a garden.

4 By Things That "Just Happen"

a. *if you let them*
    The nursery man gets inspired.
    Neighbors and relatives do it with gifts.
    You fill it with random specimens from the roadside vendor.
    Raise the house 43 inches off the ground when you build.
b. *if you can afford them*
    Plant lots of grass.
    Install a sprinkler system.
    Buy all the "labor saving" tools and gadgets, instead of getting rid of the lawn.

Of course, there is no guarantee that these items are foolproof. You will be working against nature, who is a pretty formidable adversary, unless you want to just trail along. You may also have special conditions—like a panoramic view, or an old stone quarry filled with spring water, or a little breeze that drifts across the lake on August afternoons—which you just cannot do much about.

Oh well, no one can hold off the tide indefinitely. But you sure do make it *seem* that way, Ozymandias.

Index

Page numbers in *italic* type refer to subject matter illustrated in photographs. Page numbers in roman type refer to subjects in text or captions.

Index (Continued)

Credits

The quotation on page 168 is reprinted by permission of the publishers from Sigfried Giedion's SPACE, TIME AND ARCHITECTURE, Third Edition, Cambridge, Mass.: Harvard University Press. Copyright 1941, 1949, 1954 by The President and Fellows of Harvard College.

The illustration page 43, top, courtesy of the New York Public Library Picture Collection.

PUBLICATIONS

Architectural Forum: 66–67B, 69, 70b, 74–77
Good Housekeeping: 52, 56, 58–9
House Beautiful: 54T
Ladies Home Journal: 10
McCalls: 96, 100
The New York Times: 90, 91B, 187, 191T,L&R
Progressive Architecture: 114–15, 118, 124–25, 145

PHOTOGRAPHERS

Freedman, Lionel: 106–07, 113–15, 118, 120, 122–23, 126–27, 130–31, 172T
Gottscho-Schleisner: 52, 53B, 55, 58T, 179R
Hedrich-Blessing: 60–65
Pratt, Richard: 18, 27, 37
Rosenthal, Herbert M.: 152, 154–57, 159, 160B, 161, 166, 167B, 182
Rothstein, Arthur: 85B, 101
Sherwood, Maggi: 176, 177B, 185T, 192T, 193, 205
Shulman, Julius: 66, 67B, 69–71, 74–77, 180T, 186T, 188BR
Stoller, Ezra: 2, 11–15, 23, 30–35, 56–57, 58B, 59, 86–89, 96, 100–03, 132–33, 139, 140T, 141–43, 145–51, 153, 158, 160T, 162–64, 165T, 167T, 172B, 175B, 177B, 178T, 186B, 188M, 189M&B, 190TL&B, 192B, 194–95
Wasco, Lonnie: 79–84, 85T, 91T, 92–95, 108–09, 112, 116–17, 119, 121, 124–25, 128–29, 135, 138, 140B, 144, 165B, 172M, 175T, 178B, 179L, 180B, 181, 183–84, 185B, 188T&BL, 189T, 190TR, 191B

Key: T-top, B-bottom, M-middle, L-left, R-right